Rhyme and Reason in Reading and Spelling

Rhyme and Reason
in Reading and Spelling

Lynette Bradley, Ph.D.

Fellow, International Academy for Research
    in Learning Disabilities
Department of Experimental Psychology
University of Oxford

Peter Bryant, Ph.D.

Watts Professor of Psychology
Fellow, International Academy for Research
    in Learning Disabilities
Department of Experimental Psychology
University of Oxford

**International Academy for Research in Learning Disabilities
Monograph Series, Number 1**

Ann Arbor   The University of Michigan Press

Library of Congress Cataloging in Publication Data

Bradley, Lynette, 1936–
  Rhyme and reason in reading and spelling.

  (International Academy for Research in Learning
Disabilities monograph series; no. 1)
  Summaries in English, French, German, and Spanish.
  Bibliography: p.
  1. Reading (Primary) 2. Spelling ability. 3. Rhyme—
Ability testing.   4. Alliteration—Ability testing.
5. Auditory perception—Evaluation. 6. Learning
disabilities.   I. Bryant, Peter, 1937–   .   II. Title.
III. Series.
LB1525.B73   1985   372.6   84-24153
ISBN 0-472-08055-5 (pbk.)

This series of monographs published under the sponsorship of the International Academy for Research in Learning Disabilities is dedicated to the recognition of Professor Alexander Romanovich Luria, Ph.D., of the Union of Soviet Socialist Republics, a world-class professional whose work underscores a major development in an understanding of the neurophysiological development of learning disabled children and adults.

Contents

Abstract

The aim of our project was to test a causal hypothesis about children's successes and failures in learning to read and write. We had already established that many children with learning difficulties are insensitive to rhyme and alliteration. Our hypothesis was that children's experiences with rhyme and alliteration, which typically begin some time before they arrive at school, do have an influence on the progress they make in learning how to read and spell during their first years at school.

We adopted two methods to test this hypothesis. One was longitudinal. We tested just over four hundred children of four and five years on their ability to detect rhyme and alliteration and then followed their progress in reading and spelling over the next three to four years. We found that our initial rhyming and alliteration scores bore a consistent and significant relationship to progress in reading and spelling even after the influence of intelligence and differing verbal levels had been removed. On the other hand there was no consistent relationship of this sort between the rhyming and alliteration scores and the children's progress in mathematics. These results established a definite and specific relationship between the preschool skill of recognizing rhyme and alliteration and later reading and spelling.

Our second method ensured that this relationship was a causal one. We trained some children how to categorize words by their sounds (rhyming and alliteration) and others to categorize the same words into conceptual categories. Both forms of training improved reading and spelling, but the former had a more powerful effect than the latter. We conclude that there is a causal relationship between a child's rhyming ability and her ability to read and spell, and that the difficulties which some children have with learning to read may in some cases be attributed to a failure to master a phonological skill that comes naturally to most children.

Abstrakt

Das Ziel unseres Projektes war die kausale Hypothese über Erfolg und Misserfolg von Kindern beim Erlernen von Lesen und Schreiben zu untersuchen. Wir hatten bereits festgestellt, dass viele Kinder mit Lernschwierigkeiten auf Reim und Alliteration nicht reagieren. Unsere Hypothese war, dass das Erlebnis von Reim und Alliteration bei Kindern typischerweise einige Zeit vor dem Schulanfang beginnt und Einfluss auf den Fortschritt des Erlernens von Lesen, Buchstabieren und Orthographie hat.

Wir benutzten zwei Methoden um diese Hypotese zu untersuchen. Eine war eine longitudinale. Wir untersuchten mehr als vier hundert Kinder von vier bis fünf Jahren über ihre Fähigkeit Reim und Alliteration zu entdecken, dann verfolgten wir ihren Fortschritt im Lesen, Buchstabieren und Orthographie über die nächsten drei bis vier Jahre. Wir fanden, dass unsere Reim- und Alliterationsergebnisse eine konsistente und bedeutsame Beziehung zum Fortschritt im Lesen, Buchstabieren und Orthographie hatten, sogar wenn der Einfluss von Intelligenz und unterschiedlichen verbalen Stufen berücksichtigt wurden. Auf der anderen Seite war keine konsistente Beziehung zwischen Reim- und Alliterations ergebnissen und dem Fortschritt der Kinder in Mathematik festzustellen. Diese Ergebnisse zeigen eine deutliche und spezifische Beziehung zwischen der Fähigkeit des Erkennens von Reim und Alliteration im Vorschulalter und der späteren Fähigkeit des Lesens, Buchstabierens, und Orthographie.

Unsere zweite Untersuchung bestatigte, dass diese Beziehung eine Kausale war. Wir unterrichteten einige Kinder

Worte durch ihren Laut (Reim und Alliteration) zu klassifi-
zieren und andere die gleichen Worte in begriffliche Katego-
rien einzuteilen. Beide Arten von Training verbesserte Lesen,
Buchstabieren und Orthographie, aber die erste Methode
hatte einen stärkeren Effekt als die zweite. Wir folgern dar-
aus, dass eine kausale Beziehung zwischen der Reim-Fähigkeit
eines Kindes und der Fähigkeit zu lesen, buchstabieren und
orthographisch zu schreiben besteht und dass die Schwierig-
keiten, die einige Kinder mit dem Lesen-Lernen haben in eini-
gen Fällen dem Mangel eine phonologische Kenntniss zu be-
herrschen, die bei den meisten Kindern natürlich vorhanden
ist, zuzuschreiben ist.

Résumé

Notre projet avait pour but de mettre à l'épreuve une hypothèse de causalité concernant les échecs et les réussites dans l'alphabétisation des enfants. Nous avions déjà constaté que beaucoup d'enfants éprouvant des difficultés d'apprentissage étaient insensibles à la rime et à l'allitération. Nous avons formulé l'hypothèse selon laquelle l'expérience de la rime et de l'allitération, qui commence en général un certain temps avant la scolarisation, a une influence effective sur les progrès des enfants en orthographe et en lecture pendant les premières années de la scolarité.

Nous avons adopté deux méthodes pour tester cette hypothèse. L'une était longitudinale. Nous avons testé un peu plus de quatre cents enfants âgés de quatre et cinq ans quant à leur capacité de détecter la rime et l'allitération; ensuite nous avons suivi leurs progrès en orthographe et en lecture pendant les trois ou quatre années suivantes. Nous avons trouvé que les scores du début en rime et en allitération maintenaient une relation conséquente et significative avec les progrès faits en orthographe et en lecture même après qu'on eut fait abstraction de l'influence de l'intelligence et des niveaux différents d'aptitude verbale. Par contre aucune relation conséquente du même type n'a été constatée entre les scores en rime et en allitération et les progrès des enfants en mathématiques. Ces résultats ont indiqué une relation précise et indéniable entre la capacité pré-scolaire de reconnaître la rime et l'allitération et la performance ultérieure en orthographe et en lecture.

Notre deuxième méthode nous a assurés que nous avions affaire à une relation causale. Nous avons entraîné certains

enfants à catégoriser des mots par leurs sons (rime et allitération) et d'autres enfants à répartir les mêmes mots en
catégories conceptuelles. Les deux entraînements ont eu pour
résultat une amélioration de l'orthographe et de la lecture,
mais celui-là a eu un effet plus marqué que celui-ci. Nous
avons conclu qu'il existe une relation causale entre la capacité
d'un enfant de rimer et sa capacité de lire et d'épeler des mots,
et que les difficultés qu'éprouvent certains enfants dans leur
apprentissage de l'orthographe et de la lecture pourraient dans
certains cas être attribuables à la non-acquisition d'une compé-
tence phonologique que la plupart des enfants acquièrent
spontanément.

Sumario

El propósito de nuestro proyecto fue el de comprobar una hipótesis causal sobre los éxitos y fracasos en el aprendizaje de la lectura y la ortografía que experimentan los niños. Con anterioridad habíamos establecido que muchos niños con dificultades de aprendizaje son incapaces de percibir la rima y la aliteración. De allí nuestra hipótesis de que las experiencias de los niños con la rima y la aliteración—experiencias que generalmente occuren en la etapa previa a su educacción formal, tipicamente—influyen en el ritmo de su progreso en aprender a leer y deletrear durante sus primeros años de escuela.

Se adoptaron dos métodos para comprobar la hipótesis. El primero fue longitudinal: medimos la aptitud para la detección de rima y alitercíón de más de cuatrociento niños de cuatro y cinco años de edad. Durante los próximos tres a cuatro años, seguimos el progreso que demostraban en la lectura y la ortografía. Vimos que había una relación consistente y significativa entre los puntajes iniciales en la habilidad de discriminar la rima y la aliteración, y el progreso mostrado en aprender a leer y deletrear, aún despues de restar los efectos de la inteligencia y de los diferentes niveles verbales des los niños. Por otra parte, no había ninguna relación consistente de este tipo entre la capacidad medida para la rima y la aliteración, y el progreso de los niños en matemáticas. Estos resultados establecieron una relación específica y en definitiva entre la capacidad preescolar de reconocer la rima y la aliteración, y el progreso subsiguiente en la lectura y la ortografía.

El segundo método aseguro la causalidad de la relación ya mencionada. A algunos niños les enseñamos a clasificar palabras por su sonido (por su rima y aliteración), y a otros niños les dimos métodos conceptuales para categorizar las mismas palabras. Las dos formas de enseñanza contribuyeron a mejorar el progreso de los niños en la lectura y la ortografía, pero la aplicación del primer esquema fue más efectivo que la aplicación del segundo. Por consiguiente, concluimos que existe una relación causal entre la aptitud del niño para la rima y la aliteración, y su capacidad para la lectura y la ortografía, y que las dificultades que algunos niños tienen en el aprendizaje de la lectura puedan atribuirse, en algunos casos, a un fracaso en la asimilación de una destreza fonológica que está presente en forma natural en la mayoría de los niños.

Preface

We believe that there can be no satisfactory account of learning difficulties until something definite can be said about their causes. We are also sure that nothing can be said about the causes of learning difficulties until we know something about the causes of learning. What is it, we want to know, that determines how well children learn from what they are taught at school? We started our study with the conviction that most causal hypotheses about human development had not been tested at all adequately. Our main concern was to find a better way.

The project began in March, 1978. Five rather grueling years later we are at its end. Our data are massive, and, we believe, exciting. This monograph reports our main results.

No research team is an island: no one works in isolation. But longitudinal research in particular has a way of involving a tremendous variety of other people. Our first debt is to the local schools and nurseries. Their support was essential: it came unstintingly. To be visited by outsiders over and over again, dozens and dozens of times, is an imposition however well meaning the intruders are and however willing the children seem to be carted off and asked once more about the sounds of words. Yet the schools in which we worked were so generous that we often found it hard to realize what a burden we were to them.

Generosity in another form came from the Social Science Research Council (S.S.R.C.) of the United Kingdom. It supported the project from beginning to end, and it responded flexibly to our changing and increasing demands. We had not realized what a daunting task we had set ourselves, and when we needed extra help the S.S.R.C. was there to give it.

Part of that help came in the shape of Morag Maclean, a tireless and timely worker. She kept the central task of gathering the data going very well, and when that was all in she played a major part in planning and executing its analysis. We knew that she would work well with the children. We had not realized that her relationship with the computer would be as vibrant.

The analysis seemed to employ a cast of millions. Certainly the whole of our department appeared to be sitting on the edge of its collective chair waiting to know what had happened, but some became more deeply involved than that. Ivor Lloyd, our efficient computer officer, saw us through several upheavals and trained us well. He managed—something rare in computer experts—to make us feel competent. We received some acute statistical advice from Andy Heath, and he too helped us with our computing.

All the help which we received was magnificent, but most magnficent of all was the contribution of the children themselves. We think we have found out something that will help the successors of the children who endured our questions so cheerfully, and we know that that would please them.

CHAPTER 1

A Preschool Skill of Some Significance

Our Aim

Many teachers and psychologists, concerned with the reasons for pupils' successes or failures at school, have wondered about the significance of the skills children acquire long before they go to school. The relative importance of experiences and developments which happen early in childhood is still the center of a lively debate (Clarke and Clarke 1976).

By and large the claims that have been made for the importance of these early skills have been rather general in nature. It has been argued that the child's linguistic experiences, opportunities for informal experience with the environment, or the quality of the interactions between the child's parents play a crucial role.

These are all plausible hypotheses, but they have one common weakness. They provide us with no specific mechanism. One can see in broad terms how each type of preschool experience might have a general effect, but a precise and detailed pathway from the early experience to the actual details of solving a particular problem, or acquiring a particular skill at school, is never given to us. When one gets down to what children actually do when they learn to read words or do sums, it is hard to find any precise statement about exactly how and at what point this or that preschool experience does take effect.

Yet in principle there is no reason why we should not be able to make very specific statements about the precise ways in which particular kinds of preschool experience might influence very specific educational skills. Any statement of this sort would of course help us to find better ways of preparing young children for school and perhaps of preventing some forms of learning difficulty. It would also provide us with better ways of making predictions about individual children's likely progress when they get to school and about the kind of school tasks which they might find especially difficult (or especially easy).

Our aim in this monograph is to outline a hypothesis about a very specific connection between a particular, easily measured preschool skill and a particular educational achievement. The preschool skill that interests us is the detection of rhyme and alliteration: the educational achievement is learning to read and to spell.

Rhyme and Alliteration: The Categorization of Sounds

Two questions confront anyone trying to find out how people handle the sounds of their language. One concerns the differences, the other the similarities, between words. Of the two the first is by far the more familiar and indeed the more obvious question. We know that a child has to tell words apart by their different sounds when he learns to speak and to understand speech, and we also know a great deal about how he does make these discriminations (Walk 1981).

Much less is known about the second question. Its importance has only recently been recognized. There is not a great deal in the way of empirical research to tell us when or how children begin to recognize that the words they discriminate have sounds in common. We know little about how they realize that words that sound quite different and mean quite different things sometimes either start or end with the same sounds.

Yet examples of children's contacts with this type of categorization are common. We are in fact talking about rhyme and alliteration. Words rhyme because they have sounds in common. To recognize that two words rhyme is to put them into the same category on the basis of that shared sound.

Rhymes are a natural part of a young child's life. They take up a significant part of the word games that children and parents play with each other, and indeed that children play with each other. They provide us with a very good example of a skill that children acquire informally and quite naturally long before they go to school. That skill—the capacity to categorize words on the basis of common sounds—is the central topic of our monograph. We shall try to make two main points. One is that the skill is formed before the child goes to school, and the other that it has a significant effect on his progress at school once he arrives there.

Early Rhyming

On the first point, there was when we started remarkably little evidence to be found. Some of the most striking of the evidence that did exist came from informal observations (Chukovsky 1963; Slobin 1978; Vihman 1981; Horgan 1981). Slobin reports that his three-year-old daughter made the following striking remarks: "Eggs are deggs. Enough-duff. More-bore." She was plainly attending to the words' consitituent sounds. Many other examples of the same kind of attention are to be found in Chukovsky's justly famous book *From Two to Five*. It is full of examples of neatly rhyming poems created, with evident relish, by very young children. Here are four examples of some three- and four-year-old children's verses.

> Give me, give me, before I die
> Lots and lots of potato pie
>
> I'm a whale.
> This is my tail
>
> I'm a big, big rider
> You're smaller than a spider.

I'm a flamingo
Look at my wingo

The red house
Made of strouss

The last example is particularly interesting because the
three-year-old girl was actually talking about straw, but bent
that word to make it rhyme with *house*. Rhyme took prece-
dence, and Chukovsky gives us other examples of the same
thing. One is a poem by a two-and-a-half year old.

The duckling and the big goose
Sat on the broken sail-oose

Here is a dramatic example of the importance of rhyme to
young children. Not only do they recognize rhyme and produce rhyming sentences with ease, they also change the very
form of words that they know to suit the rules of rhyme. It is
quite plain that these children know a great deal about categorizing words by their sounds.

There is as well a little evidence that young children are
able to detect rhymes as well as to produce them. Lenel and
Cantor (1981) showed that children as young as four are quite
good at saying whether two words rhyme or not, and Read
(1978) had quite striking success with children of the same age
who were given an amusing rhyming game. It involved puppets with particular names: these puppets liked words that
rhymed with their names ("Would Ed like bed or bead?"
"food or fed?"). Most of the kindergarten children in Read's
study managed to play this game with very little difficulty.

All in all, despite the fact that this quite remarkable achievement on the part of young children has been all but ignored by
child psychologists, it is fair to assume that children are aware
of rhymes, dabble in them, enjoy them, and probably learn a
great deal from them about the phonological structure of their

language—and all this long before they go to school. We can turn now to the question of the significance of this skill when they do become schoolchildren.

This is not a new question, and of course the few people who have looked at rhyme in young children have wondered about the long-term significance of what they were studying. Chukovsky (1956) himself probably made the most extreme claim.

> Rhyme-making during the second year of life is an inescapable stage of our linguistic development. Children who do not perform such linguistic exercises are abnormal or ill. These activities are indeed exercises, and it is difficult to think of a more rational system in phonetics than such frequent repetition of all possible sound variations. (P. 64)

But statements like this tell us nothing specific about the connections between a child's awareness of rhyme and the skills he has to acquire later on at school. Yet there is a very specific connection to be made, and it is to this that we now turn.

Rhyme, Alliteration, and Learning to Read

There are, in our view, two good reasons for making a connection between a child's preschool experiences with rhyme and alliteration and his eventual success at learning to read and write. The first is that both activities depend on breaking words and syllables into phonological segments.

To rhyme is to see and use the similarity between words like *cat* and *hat* or between *light* and *fight*. Understanding that *cat* and *hat* have a sound in common (-*at*) must involve breaking up both words into at least two phonological segments—*c* and *at*, and *h* and *at*. Exactly the same argument must be applied to alliteration, in which words like *cat* and *cap* are seen to be the same. Rhyme and alliteration must involve an explicit, conscious understanding of the phonological segments in words.

So must learning the alphabet. The alphabet works by breaking words into phonological segments. Each letter represents a unit of sound that is usually a great deal smaller than a word or a syllable. There is no possible way in which a child could understand and use the alphabetic principle with any degree of success without being able to isolate and manipulate such phonological segments.

Thus when the two-, three-, or four-year-old child produces poems or strings of rhyming words, and when he enjoys a poem read to him by his parents or a game with them that involves rhyme ("round and round the garden . . . ," "pata-cake patacake baker's man") he may very well be exercising and developing a skill that will stand him in very good stead when he has to cope with written language several years later.

This is not all. The third possible link between rhyming and learning to read and write concerns categorization. Rhyming and alliteration, as we have seen, involve putting words into categories on the basis of common sounds. So, again, does written language. Words like *light* and *fight* have both sounds and spelling patterns in common. It follows that children learn how to group words, when they rhyme, in a way that will help them when they begin to learn to read and spell.

These two connections are plausible enough, and they have the distinct advantage of a clear and coherent pathway, but they are still speculative. One can see exactly how one specific activity could very well affect the other equally specific activity later on. But one still needs to demonstrate that such effects actually do happen.

The fact is that, though little enough is known about children's awareness of rhyme and alliteration, even less has been established about its causal links with learning to read and write. There are a number of reasons for this dearth of empirical evidence, but the main one is the general difficulty of establishing causal connections in child development.

The idea of a causal link between early rhyming and success in reading is certainly not a new one. Savin (1972), for example, wrote a well-known paper asserting that poor readers are typically weak at word games and insensitive to rhyme. In much the same vein Vihman (1981, 319), a linguist, stated her assumption that children's experience of detecting the phonological similarity between words "underlies pre-reading and writing skills."

These are arresting claims, but none is backed by hard evidence. Vihman simply states an assumption. The conclusions of the Bullock committee were influential, but were based on speculations. Indeed the report makes a comment about the need for research on the effects of rhyme and word games (Bullock 1975). Even Savin, whose paper was based on his experiences with poor readers, simply reports general impressions: his evidence is not even anecdotal.

We have to look quite hard to find any relevant data, and when we do we are immediately faced with the very great problems of establishing in a convincing way the existence of causal links in child development.

Relational Studies of the Connection between Rhyming Skills and Learning to Read

Most of the relevant studies deal in relations. They look at the relations between children's rhyming skills and their reading ability. One way to plot this sort of relation is to use correlations. Calfee, Chapman, and Venezky (1972), for example, reported a strong relationship between children's reading achievement at the end of their first year at school and their success in a rhyming task. But, for reasons which hardly need review, results such as these are not on their own at all convincing. Correlations by themselves tell us little about causes. In this particular study both the skills, rhyming and reading, might have been determined by some unknown third factor. There may be no causal connection here at all.

Exactly the same criticism has to be made about another set of studies that plots the relationship between rhyming skills and reading, but in a different way. These are the studies that measure the rhyming skill of backward readers and compare them to normal readers of the same age. It has been reported that backward readers manage rhyming tasks a great deal less effectively than do other children of the same age and intelligence (Audley 1976), a result that certainly supports Savin's earlier assertion. But here again cause and effect cannot be disentangled. The problem is one of direction of cause and effect, which is a familiar problem in any relational study. The children's poor rhyming skills could have led to their slow progress in reading, but there is the equally plausible alternative that the children's relatively poor reading levels could account for their insensitivity to rhyme. It could be the child's reading level that determines his skill with rhyme, rather than the other way round.

In fact this difficulty is all too common in studies of backwardness in reading. The traditional design, a very weak one, has taken the form of comparing backward and normal readers of the same age and intellectual level, and of looking for some deficit among the backward readers. Whenever a difference between the two groups—usually a difference that favors the normal readers—is discovered, the experimenters conclude that they may have isolated a cause of the backward readers' difficulty.

The trouble with this design is that it leaves the question of cause and effect up in the air. The two groups, equal in chronological age and mental age, have reached different reading levels. The reading level of the backward readers is, perforce, a great deal the lower of the two. So it is quite possible that any difference that emerges between the two groups could be the product of the difference in reading levels. Yet this alternative has been all but ignored by the many people who have stuck so resolutely to this unsatisfactory type of design. This point has been made in a number of papers (Bradley and Bryant 1978, 1979; Bryant and Bradley 1980; Snowling 1980; Frith and Snowling 1983), and a recent and influential book on reading problems (Vellutino 1979) has shown the weaknesses of many of the experiments that made this traditional kind of comparison.

It is a problem that can be solved. The solution is to compare backward and normal readers at the same level of reading. Simply design a study that compares backward and normal readers whose reading ages are the same. Both groups will be of normal intelligence, and both will have reached the same reading level. But the normal readers will have got there earlier than the backward readers and so will be younger.

The great advantage of this design is that it rules out the possibility that any difference that emerges between normal and backward readers is the product of a discrepancy in reading levels. That could not be: the reading levels are the same. Therefore if a study of this sort does demonstrate a weakness in backward readers, that weakness could not possibly be a product of their low reading level. With a result of this sort one may indeed have isolated a cause.

It is a matter of some interest, as Frith and Snowling (1983) have recently pointed out, that the inspiration behind this solution comes from much earlier research by people concerned with mental retardation who encountered a very similar problem. O'Connor and Hermelin (1963), in their search for qualitative differences between retardates and normal children, had to find a control for the quantitative intellectual differences between the two populations. Their idea, now very widely adopted, was to equate the two groups—retardates and normal controls—in terms of absolute intellectual level. The two groups had the same mental age, though of course a very different chronological age. Five-year-old normal children with a mental age of five years would be compared to ten-year-old retarded children whose mental age was also at the five-year level. Any differences that emerged between the two groups could not be a direct product of the backwardness of the retarded group, since the two group's intellectual levels were the same. Once this advance had been made the way was clear to apply the same strategy of research to other groups. Frith (1970), for example, and Hermelin and O'Connor (1970) themselves went on to compare autistic children to other groups with the same absolute intellectual levels with striking results. Naturally it became clear that the same strategy of looking at the problems of a group deficient in some quality by comparing them to normal people who in absolute terms were at the same level as far as that quality is concerned was appropriate for the study of reading backwardness.

A number of people adopted this design for studying backward readers. We ourselves carried out just such a study several years ago (Bradley and Bryant 1978). It involved a large group of backward readers, all of whom were in normal schools. Their intelligence levels were average or above. No clear evidence existed that any of their learning difficulties were the product of emotional, physical, or social handicaps. They were compared to a younger group of children who read normally for their age and whose reading levels were the same as those of the backward reading group. The details of the two groups are presented in table 1.

We gave the children in both groups two types of tasks. One involved detecting rhyme and alliteration, and the other producing rhyme. In the detection task we said four words at a time, all but one of which shared a common sound. The child's task was to spot that word—to tell us which was the odd word out. Sometimes the common sound that the odd word did not share was the opening consonant (e.g., "sun, sea, sock, rag"),

TABLE 1.   Details of the Two Groups

	Backward Readers ($N = 60$)	Normal Readers ($N = 30$)
Mean age	10y 4m	6y 10m
Mean I.Q. (W.I.S.C.)	108.7	107.9
Mean reading age	7y 7m	7y 6m
Mean spelling age	6y 10m	7y 2m

sometimes the middle vowel ("nod, red, fed, bed"), and sometimes the end consonant ("weed, peel, need, deed"). Notice that the first of these three conditions deals in alliteration, and the other two in rhyme.

Table 2 shows what happened in the detection task. The backward readers did not fare at all well. Despite the fact that they were older and more advanced intellectually, and despite the fact that both tests involved only spoken words, their scores were a great deal worse than those of the normal readers. All three conditions produced this difference, but of the three the alliteration condition, which was generally the hardest, also put the backward readers at a particular disadvantage in comparison to the other group. We shall have a great deal more to say about the relative significance of alliteration and rhyme in later chapters.

In the production task we simply read out a series of words to each child, and asked the child after saying each word to think of another one that rhymed with it. The backward readers had no more luck with the production task, as table 3 shows. All in all we seemed to have shown a striking weakness among backward readers, and it was one that could not be explained as the product of their low reading levels. Our design had taken care of that.

TABLE 2.   Mean Errors Out of Six in the Sound Categorization Task

Condition	Backward Readers ($N = 60$)		Normal Readers ($N = 30$)	
	Mean	S.D.	Mean	S.D.
End letter different	1.15	1.43	0.17	1.11
Middle letter different	1.49	1.58	0.37	0.99
First letter different	2.62	2.26	0.67	1.18

S.D. = standard deviation

We concluded that we had isolated a possible cause of learning difficulties. Insensitivity to rhyme and alliteration and an inadequate understanding of how words can be grouped together on the basis of shared sounds might lead to some of the problems that beset so many children when they begin to learn to read and to spell.

Important as this conclusion seemed, we knew that it had one limitation. To isolate a cause of backwardness in reading is one thing: to establish that the same factor determines progress in reading in the population at large is quite another. The trouble is that backward readers are by definition an unusual group of children. The connection which we have established in backward readers between rhyming and reading may be something entirely to do with them. We cannot be sure that it holds for other children too.

So, even after our own experiment had been completed, we had to conclude that, in general, studies that related children's sensitivity to rhyme to their progress in learning to read had not yet established anything definite about cause and effect in the normal run of readers. But this, we knew, did not exhaust

TABLE 3.   Frequency of the Number of Children Who Failed to Produce a Rhyme in Any of the Six Rhyme Production Trials

Number of Trials	Backward Readers (N = 62)	Normal Readers (N = 31)
0	37	28
1	4	1
2	4	0
3	4	0
4	4	0
5	2	2
6	2	0
7	2	0
8	0	0
9	0	0
10	3	0

all the possibilities. Traditionally relational studies have provided us with only one of our two main sources of evidence about causes in development. The other source is the training study.

Training Studies

The rationale of training studies is quite different from that of the relational study. Let us say that the experimenter's aim is to test the hypothesis that a certain type of experience (A) brings about a particular developmental change (B). The idea of the training experiment is to test the hypothesis by giving an experimental group extra experience with A and seeing if, as a result, that group scores more highly in tests of B than does a control group not having the benefit of added experience with A. If that happens the experimenters usually conclude that they have demonstrated that A does, at least to some extent, determine B.

It is by no means a watertight rationale, as we shall see, but before we go into its weaknesses we should note that there do not seem to have been any conclusive studies of the effect on reading of training children how to produce or to detect rhyme more effectively. There have, it is true, been several attempts to develop phonological skills and to look at the effects of this training on children's reading. However, either these did not involve rhyme at all (Zhurova 1973; Goldstein 1976), or they combined rhyming with other forms of phonological analysis (Olofsson and Lundberg, 1983).

When we began to look at the possibility of rhyming skills being a causal determinant of learning to read, we did not know whether training children to handle rhyme and alliteration would help them to learn to read and write. Even if there had been studies of this sort, studies that involved training in rhyming and nothing else, we should not have been able to draw any definite conclusion about the causal influence of rhyming skills from them. Training studies, we realized, had their weaknesses too, and the most serious of these seemed to us to be their artificiality.

The trouble is that it is perfectly possible to train a skill successfully in the laboratory in a way that has nothing what-ever to do with what happens in the real world and particularly with what takes place in the classroom. With a training study you would run the risk, for example, of finding that improving children's rhyming skills does lead to greater success in reading in your experiment, even if no link between these two things did exist outside your own laboratory.

The training study certainly has its strengths. It can be used, for example, to evaluate new teaching methods. In a limited way, it is even good at isolating causes. Provided that the control groups are right, you can be reasonably sure that any effect in a training experiment is a causal one. But you can be sure of it only within your experimental setting. Outside, it is quite another matter.

This means that, as far as we have gone, we are entitled to one solid conclusion only about the significance of children's early rhyming skills. There definitely is a link between these skills and the problems of children who turn out to be back-ward readers. There are, however, other ways of looking at phonological skills in young children, and other phonological skills to look at. The relationship between these and learning to read and write has received a great deal of attention. Up to now we have talked only about rhyme and alliteration. Let us turn now to the way in which children deal with other phono-logical tasks.

Phonological Awareness and Learning to Read and Write

Broadly speaking there are two questions to ask. One is whether young children are able to recognize phonological segments before they learn to read, and the other whether their skill at doing so affects their progress in learning to read.

We have already seen that rhyming studies give something of a positive answer to the second question, at any rate as far as backward readers are concerned. What about studies which use other phonological tasks?

These tend to be markedly more pessimistic about young children's phonological skills than studies of rhyming. We have already seen how the ease and enjoyment with which young children take to rhyme suggests very strongly that they are aware of phonological segments long before they begin to read. But other techniques designed to measure children's "phonological awareness" have painted an entirely different picture. The reason for this discrepancy is almost certainly the clumsiness of the experiments, in which young children flounder, rather than in the ineptitude of the children themselves.

One of the commonest techniques is to ask children to subtract sounds from words. The idea came originally from Bruce (1964). He simply asked children, to take one example, what the word *stand* would sound like if the *t* sound was removed, or, to take another example, what would become of the word *penny* without the *y* sound.

This turned out to be an extremely difficult task, and one with which children as old as seven and eight years, children who had already made considerable progress in reading and writing, were often completely at sea. But their difficulties need not surprise us. The task makes a lot of other demands besides breaking words into segments. It involves subtraction, which a lot of children find quite difficult. It also may depend on the children being able to visualize the word in its written form: in other words the ability to manage this task might be a product of learning to read and nothing very much to do with the child's initial phonological skills.

Indeed, this latter possibility has some empirical backing. Morais, Cary, Alegria, and Bertelson (1979) compared a group of illiterate adults in Portugal to another group who could read: apparently illiteracy is common enough in that country for two such groups to be comparable in every other respect apart from the fact that one had the chance to learn to read and the other did not. In this study the two groups were given a task rather similar to Bruce's, and it turned out to be very much more difficult for the illiterate group than for the other people. The experimenters concluded that phonological awareness is the product of learning to read. This conclusion, at any rate in its broadest form, is almost certainly wrong. If children can detect and produce rhymes as young as they do, phonological awareness in some form must precede reading. But the study certainly does suggest that the kind of awareness studied in Bruce's task not only follows learning to read but is actually caused by it. We must bear in mind that there may be different levels of awareness of sounds in words, and one level might precede and determine learning to read while another might follow and be determined by the same learning.

Much the same kind of problem encountered with Bruce's technique besets another common way of looking at children's phonological awareness. These are the well-known tapping experiments, conducted by Liberman and her colleagues (Liberman, Shankweiler, Liberman, Fowler, and Fischer 1978). They devised two tasks, one a "syllable," the other a "phoneme" task. In the syllable task they would say a series of words and the child had to learn how to tap out the number of syllables in each of those words: one tap for *bus,* two for *bedtime,* and so on. The child had to tap, too, in the phoneme task, but here he learned to tap out the word's phonemes instead. So, three taps would be needed for *bus*—a three-phoneme word—in this task.

Liberman and her colleagues tried to get five- and six-year-old children to learn both tasks, and found that the syllable task was by far the easier of the two. Indeed a large number of children made no progress at all in the phoneme task. The experimenters concluded that the phoneme is not a natural unit for the young child who is just beginning to learn to read, and they argued that this unawareness of phonemes constitutes a hurdle for most young children at the time that they begin to come to grips with written language.

Once again we must protest on behalf of the children. To conclude that they are not normally aware of phonemes from an experiment like this would surely be an act of considerable perversity. Tapping, after all, is a rhythmic task and the rhythm of a word is captured in its syllables, not in its phonemes. It is no surprise at all that the syllable task is much the easier of the two. The difference might have nothing to do with isolating phonemes. It may simply be that children see the task as a rhythmic one and turn to syllables rather than to phonemes. In fact Liberman and Shankweiler (1976) report that others have found much the same results in a nonrhythmic version of their phoneme task, in which the children had to put out tokens instead of tapping. But here again there are other difficulties. The new version involves one-to-one correspondence, which is notoriously difficult for young children. We cannot say what the effects of this extra cognitive hurdle will be.

Still other techniques have been used to test children's phonological skills, but most of these seem as dubious to us as the two we have already described. One is the use of jokes that turn on phonological themes. Hirsh-Pasek, Gleitman, and Gleitman (1978), for example, showed that children find jokes about phonological distortions (Question: "What do you get if you put some ducks in a box?" Answer: "A box of quackers.") less amusing than, for example, puns. But this difference could easily be explained in a number of different ways. Children are probably more familiar with puns, which often have a phonological twist anyway, and they might detect and understand the distortion in Hirsh-Pasek's phonological jokes without finding it particularly funny.

There is also a well-known experiment by Fox and Routh (1975) that does seem to show quite considerable phonological skills in young children whose ages ranged from three to six years. But even their results may well be an underestimate of what young children could in principle manage in phonological tasks. Their way of testing a child's awareness of phonemes was to say a one-syllable word, like *Pete,* and then to ask the child to say "just a little bit" of the word back to them.

They found that even three-year-old children could identify and segment some of the phonemes in the words they heard, and that the four year olds were able to do it correctly more than 50 percent of the time.

These are considerable successes and they come at a comparatively early age. They come, too, in the face of instructions that must have been unclear to these very young children. "Just a little bit" need not mean a phoneme, and it is very difficult to see what it could mean to a young child unless he has an explicit concept of what a phoneme or an alphabetic letter is.

We are faced, then, with a series of studies that try to establish that preschool children are dimly aware, or not aware at all, of phonemes, but that, in the end, fail completely to demonstrate that this hurdle actually does exist. The only convincing evidence to come out of these experiments suggests that even three-year-old children can break words and syllables into smaller units of sound. This agrees with research on rhyming in young children, but, to date, the amount of evidence from all sources is painfully thin. We can conclude that children are aware of phonemes long before they go to school, but we can conclude it only very tentatively.

This takes us to the second question, which is whether the child's phonological skills affect his eventual success in learning to read and write. Evidence that they do comes in two forms, both of which are interesting and extremely valuable, but both in the end too indirect from the point of view of our causal question.

The first consists of a set of experiments that show quite unambiguously that children do use phonological codes when they begin to learn to read and write. This is an important point, and is certainly consistent with the hypothesis that a

child's success in learning to read will be affected by his phonological skills.

One of the major studies to make this point was a series of
experiments by Doctor and Coltheart (1980), in which the
basic technique was to use homophones. The argument was
that if children got confused over words that sounded right but
were in fact wrong they must be attending to the phonological
aspects of words which they read. The most telling condition
was when the children had to judge whether a sentence like
"She bloo up the balloon." was correct (the correct answer
was "No."). Even children as young as six had a great deal of
difficulty with this task, and much more difficulty when the
wrong word did not sound right ("She blod up the balloon."
or "She know up the balloon."). This demonstrates that young
children do pay attention to letter-sound correspondences
when they read, even when it is misleading to do so.

Another ingenious experiment by Snowling and Frith (1981)
uses a different technique to make the same point. This was a
study in which the main aim was to distinguish several different codes in reading—visual and orthographic, as well as phonological. We shall concentrate on the evidence for phonological processing. By presenting scripts in which either visual,
orthographic, or phonological cues were distorted in various
combinations the experimenters were able to show that seven-
year-old children did use the letter-sound correspondences to
read these sentences.

So far we have kept to reading, but the other major asso-
ciated activities, writing and spelling, show even stronger evidence of phonological processing. One clear piece of evidence
for this is a curious phenomenon we reported some years ago
(Bradley and Bryant 1979; Bryant and Bradley 1980). Children in the initial stages of learning to read and write seem to
keep the two activities of reading and spelling rather separate.
The evidence for this is that they read some words that they
cannot spell (not a surprising pattern since it is probably true
of most adults as well) and also that they manage to spell other

words that they cannot read. This second discrepancy—
spelling words and not reading them—is certainly surprising,
and it seems to happen mainly among beginning readers. It is
rare according to our evidence above a reading age of seven
and a half years.

On its own this odd phenomenon tells us nothing about
phonological processes, but a closer look at the words involved
does suggest a specific hypothesis about the children's depen-
dence on these processes. When we gave young children the
same words to read on some occasions and to spell on others,
we found that the words indvidual children managed to spell
and yet could not read were highly regular from a letter-sound
point of view. They were words like *bun* and *mat,* and they
were in complete contrast to the other type of discrepant
words—those which the children could read but not spell:
these tended to be words like *school* and *light,* which are difficult to build up on a single-letter-by-sound basis. This difference suggests that the children's spelling depends very closely
on letter-sound correspondences, or in other words that it is
heavily dependent on phonological processes.

This conclusion was supported by a further result. We gave
children the words that they had not read before in our tests.
These necessarily included the words they could neither read
nor spell and also the curious category of words that they
could spell but could not read. We persuaded the children to
try reading them again but this time forced them to adopt a
phonological strategy, and we found a marked improvement
but mainly with the words which they had been able to spell;
they began to read these but still failed to read the words that
they neither read nor spelled before. This suggests very
strongly that the children had been adopting a phonological
strategy in spelling, and could read words that they could spell
if adopted the same phonological strategy in reading.

Much the same point about a particularly strong connection
between spelling and phonological awareness has recently
been made by Snowling and Perin (1982). They gave children

of four and five years a phonological segmentation task in which the children had to name the constituent sounds in a set of words. They were also given reading and spelling tasks with the same words. A strong relationship was found between the phonological task and the spelling test. Reading, on the other hand, seemed not to be related to the children's success with phonological segments. The experimenters concluded that learning to spell initially depends on phonological skills to a far greater extent than does reading. In a later experiment Perin (1983) reached a similar conclusion on the basis of a very different kind of experimental design. She compared three groups of fourteen- to fifteen-year-old children: one group read and spelled normally, the second read and spelled poorly, while the third read normally but spelled poorly for its age (a common pattern among teenagers). She gave these children tasks of a phonological nature, the most striking of which was a spoonerism task: the experimenter said two words to the child who had to repeat them as a spoonerism. If he heard *Chuck Berry* he had to say *Buck Cherry*. Perin found that performance on this task was closely related to spelling, and not to reading. Both groups of poor spellers did equally badly, and much worse than the group with a normal spelling age. She concluded again that spelling involves phonological segmentation more than reading does.

Put together these studies suggest quite strongly that phonological awareness plays an important part in learning to read and perhaps an even more important part in learning to spell. This is a valuable start, but as Coltheart (1983) has pointed out it does not establish a causal connection. It shows that the two things are connected: it does not show what causes what.

Another possibility is to turn to studies of individual differences in phonological awareness and to relate these to success and failure in reading. Is there a relation between the two things? The answer as we shall see is that there is, but that this relationship tells us nothing definite about causes.

There is a wealth of evidence for the relation from longitu-

dinal studies, from comparisons of normal with backward
readers and from straight correlations between measures of
phonological skills and reading levels (Golinkoff 1978; Lundberg 1978; Vellutino 1979; Hakes, Evans, and Tunmer 1980;
Grieve, Tunmer, and Pratt 1980; Nesdale, Herriman, and
Tunmer 1980). Children's reading levels are related to their
success in Bruce's subtraction task, to the extent to which they
see the point of Hirsh-Pasek's phonological jokes, and, as we
have already noted, to their skill at detecting and producing
rhyme, as well as to several other tests of phonological awareness. All the signs are that whatever measure one takes, however imperfect it is, it nevertheless turns out to be related in
some way or other to success in reading and writing.

However, on its own, this relationship tells us very little. If
you are looking for causes, you have two reasons for caution
when you are faced with a study which only reports relations
between one skill and another. We have mentioned both
reasons already in the section on rhyming. One is that you
often cannot tell which of two related variables is affecting the
other.

Lest the thought that learning to read could be a cause of
phonological awareness rather than its result seems farfetched,
we must remind ourselves that it is a thought that has been
taken very seriously indeed by at least one team of investiga-
tors. We have already seen how Morais, Cary, Alegria, and
Bertelson (1979) concluded from their study of illiterate
people that it was their lack of experience with learning to
read that made phonological segmentation difficult for them.
The same group of experimenters (Alegria, Pignot, and Morais 1982) have also looked at children in the early stages of
learning to read, and their results led them to the same conclusion—that phonological awareness is the product of learning
to read rather than the other way round. They looked at six-
year-old children from two schools. These children had been
taught to read for four months at the time of the experiment,
but the teaching methods were very different in the two

schools; in one the teaching was on a "phonic" basis while the other school concentrated on teaching the "whole word." The test given to both groups of children consisted of a syllable task, in which the experimenters said a word of two syllables on each trial (e.g., "bofa") and the child had to repeat it with the syllables reversed ("fabo"), and a phoneme task in which the words consisted of two phonemes which the children also had to reverse ("os," "so"). The experimenters found a very big difference between the two groups in the phoneme task (the "whole word" group was worse) but no group difference in the syllable task, and concluded not only that the different educational regimes had different effects, but also that the ability to separate phonemes depends to a great extent on being taught how to do it in reading. They could very well be right about the kind of phonological skill they were testing, but we should note again that just as there are different tests of phonological awareness, so there may be different levels of this awareness. What these experimenters found with one test may not be true of other tests. However, they have produced a dramatic illustration of the way in which teaching children to read might affect their awareness of sounds in words. This work shows, in a very concrete way, that we should be particularly cautious with correlational data about reading skills and phonological awareness. They are inherently ambiguous.

Fortunately the O'Connor/Hermelin idea of matching children on the variable on which the group of interest is backward has been widely recognized as an empirical improvement in the study of reading and of reading difficulties. There are several good studies that adopt the Equal Reading Age design we outlined when we described our study of rhyme detection by backward readers. In one such study Snowling (1980) compared a group of normal readers with a group of older backward readers of normal intelligence who were matched with the normal children in terms of reading age. Thus any differences between the two groups could not be attributed to a difference in reading levels. She gave them a number of tasks

involving nonsense words and found that there was one task
that was managed very differently by the two groups. This was
a visual-auditory task in which the children were shown a nonsense word (visual presentation) on each trial and had to judge
whether it was the same as a nonsense word spoken immediately afterward. This was quite a difficult task, but for the
normal children, the higher their reading level the better they
managed it. No such relationship between reading level and
this task occurred among the backward readers. They found it
difficult whatever their absolute reading level, and made many
more mistakes on it than the normal readers did.

This is a powerful result that is reinforced by a later study
by Frith and Snowling (1983), which demonstrated that backward readers have more difficulty with reading nonsense
words, even though in this experiment the two groups read
real words equally well. The fact that backward readers have
particular difficulty with nonsense words does suggest a phonological problem. The only way these words can be decoded
is by using letter-sound correspondences, and this demands a
phonological code. Naturally these two results fit well with
those of our rhyming study described earlier. The fact that
backward readers have difficulty with phonological tasks even
when reading age is controlled seems to rule out the possiblity
that this difficulty is the product of a low level of reading. The
phonological problem is much more likely to be the cause than
the result of the backwardness in reading. These studies are
very much more powerful than mere correlations. But, as we
have already pointed out of our own study, what is true of
backward readers may not also be true of the wide range of
normal readers.

There is, too, another problem which neither these reading
age matches nor correlational studies avoid. It is the possibility
of the tertium quid—the unknown and therefore unmeasured
third factor that determines both the variables concerned. If
such a variable did exist any relation between the two variables being studied might have nothing to do with causes.

Both could be determined by the third and unmeasured variable. No study that deals in relations alone can rule out such a possibility, however many variables it measures and tries to rule out.

So the various attempts to show that phonological skills and reading go hand in hand do not tell us anything definite about causes. Even if one forgets for a moment the weaknesses of many of the tests involved, it is still quite impossible to be certain about the popular but unsecured hypothesis that a child's progress in reading will depend to a large extent on how aware he is of the phonological properties of speech.

There are, it seems, many problems. But the central problem—the difficulty at the heart of it all—is quite clear. It is the problem of how to test hypotheses about causes in child development. This is the question we must now do our best to answer.

Summary

Most hypotheses about the connection between children's preschool experiences and preschool skills and their later success or failure at school are rather general in nature. They do not suggest a specific mechanism.

We wish to suggest a specific way in which a skill that a child acquires quite naturally long before he goes to school might affect his progress in learning to read and spell. The skill we have in mind is the skill of handling rhyme and alliteration.

There is some evidence that children are aware of rhyme before they go to school, and also that many of the children who have been at school for some time and have failed to learn to read adequately are relatively insensitive to rhyme and alliteration. This suggests that rhyming skills might to some extent determine a child's success in learning to read and write.

There is a good reason for suggesting such a link. Rhyme and alliteration involve breaking words up into smaller phonological segments. So does the alphabet. Rhymes therefore might introduce the child to phonological segments and also show him how words can be grouped together on the basis of common sounds.

Although there is a good deal of evidence for some relationship between phonological skills and success in learning to read and to spell, none of it establishes a causal link. Correlational studies are unconvincing because they do not rule out the possibility of the influence of some third unknown factor. Studies of backward readers that match groups on reading age are a definite advance and have told us a great deal about the phonological problems of the backward reader. But they do not necessarily show us what the normal processes of learning to read are, and they do not rule out the tertium quid. Training studies, on their own, run the risk of artificiality. We await an adequate design for testing causes in children's development.

CHAPTER 2

A Design for All Causes

Our theory is about a skill that children acquire long before they go to school and that has a powerful influence on the way in which they learn to read and to spell. Handling rhyme and alliteration is the skill we have in mind, and we have concentrated on it because it seems to us the most natural way of learning about segments of sound. Now we want to test this causal idea.

How does one test it? So far we have discussed three methods. One is to compare backward and normal readers at the same reading level. As we have seen, this is certainly a fruitful way of finding out about the problems of children with learning difficulties; but it does not necessarily tell us much about other children. To make a more general statement we have to turn to the other two methods and, as we have seen, both have serious problems.

The other two methods are the correlation (preferably in longitudinal studies) and intervention or training study, and since they are all that is available it seems like a council of despair to argue that both are seriously flawed. If neither method on its own is at all satisfactory it is difficult at first to see how one could possibly establish any certain causal links.

There is however a simple way around the problem. Considering the two methods together reveals that their strengths and weaknesses are complementary. Where correlations are weak, intervention is strong: and exactly at the point at which intervention studies can tell us nothing correlations come into their own. It follows that combining the two is an attractive solution. One should do longitudinal studies to see whether the thing that one is interested in (say rhyming skill) does predict later success in reading, but one should also give a group of children intensive training in the skill in question and see whether it helps them to read better. This in fact is the central argument behind the design of our project, and so we must look at it in some detail.

Longitudinal correlations have one great strength and one great weakness (Bradley and Bryant 1983; Coltheart 1983). The strength is that they do establish a genuine relationship in the real world. Suppose for example that it was shown that the more skillful children are with rhyme before they go to school, the quicker they learn to read when they get there. Provided that the measures are sensitive and provided that they are administered carefully and provided too that the right steps are taken to control for other known variables such as intelligence, this result would show that there is a connection between the two skills; but (and here is the weakness) you cannot be sure that the connection is a causal one. As we have already seen, the alternative that can never be ruled out is that both skills, the early and the late skill, might be governed by some other unknown unmeasurable third factor. There is no way of saying which of these two alternatives is the right one.

It seems like an impasse until one considers the strengths and weaknesses of training studies and sees that they are precisely the opposite. Intervention is very good at establishing a causal link but quite useless when it comes to demonstrating that the link has anything to do with real life. The two methods seem to be mirror images of one another.

There is a very simple reason why a training study can definitely establish causal links, at any rate within the confines of the study itself. It can do so because it is an experiment and in experiments one can manipulate events. Suppose that you want to discover whether training in rhyming causes a change in children's reading skills. All that is needed is a properly controlled training study. Train some children in rhyming, and treat other children in the same way in every respect apart

from the experience with rhyming. Then compare the eventual
achievement of the two groups in reading. Suppose that the
first group manages in the end to read more skillfully than the
second. If all the right precautions have been taken this is a
difference which can only be explained in causal terms. The
experimental group can only have done better because the
children in it learned how to rhyme more efficiently, and for
no other reason.

So much for the advantage of this technique. Now we must
think of its main disadvantage; this, as we saw in the last
chapter, is the risk of artificiality. In a training experiment it is
quite possible to cause a change in children's behavior in a way
that has nothing at all to do with events in real life. There are
clear examples in other branches of developmental psychology.

One has only to look (Bryant 1981) at the very large number of successful attempts to train conservation. There are, it
is now well established, many different ways to train a child to
solve the conservation task. This task is designed to test young
children's understanding of the principle of invariance and
does so by asking them whether quantities have changed after
their perceptual appearance (but not their actual quantity) are
transformed. There are so many, in fact, that it seems very
probable that many of them are quite irrelevant to the way in
which children normally learn how to solve this problem. In
other words the methods used in many of the successful conservation training experiments almost certainly have very little
to do with the way in which children learn the concept in real
life. With successful training experiments like these one can be
certain that a causal link has been demonstrated, but one has
to remain quite undecided about its relevance to anything outside the laboratory. And so it must be with any other training
experiment. On its own it is bound to be inconclusive.

Now we can see why the strengths and weaknesses of the
two methods are complementary. Longitudinal correlations establish genuine relationships, but do not demonstrate causes.
Training studies establish causal links but with no guarantee

that these represent connections which really do exist outside the laboratory. Each is only one side of the causal coin. The obvious solution is to put them together.

Let us see how this would work with rhyming. To test the hypothesis that this skill does influence a child's progress in reading, we should have to do two things. One would involve longitudinal predictions: we should have to test how well a large group of children detect rhymes before learning to read. These scores could be related later to their eventual success in reading and writing. This would be a typical longitudinal study, and provided that other relevant factors such as intelligence were measured and controlled, would establish a genuine relationship between one skill and the other.

But, as we have seen, it would not establish that the link was a causal one because both skills might be regulated by some other factor. However, this unknown third variable can effectively be ruled out if the project also includes a properly designed training study. Let us assume for the moment that we find that children trained to be more sensitive to rhyme would also end up reading better: let us assume too that their reading is superior to that of children in a control group who in every other respect apart from the experience in rhyming were like the children trained to rhyme. This would surely establish that an increase in skill in handling rhymes causes a change in children's reading levels.

Together these two (entirely hypothetical) results would indeed be very good evidence for a causal argument about rhyming. If rhyming skills are shown to be related to progress in reading and if an increase in these skills is followed by an improvement in reading too, it would be very difficult to conclude anything else than that rhyming skills do influence reading.

Yet, simple and obvious as this argument seems to be, we have been hard put to find any studies that adopt the sort of design we are now advocating. Certainly in studies of reading and of reading problems people seem to have kept to one method or the other and not to have combined the two. That was why we found all previous arguments about the determinants of success in reading unconvincing. That too was why we decided to combine longitudinal and training methods in our attempt to test our hypothesis about the importance of rhyming and alliteration skills.

Summary

The strengths and weaknesses of the two main methods for testing hypotheses about cause and effect are complementary. Longitudinal correlations demostrate genuine relations, but they might not be cause-effect relations because of the problem of the unknown third factor. Training studies, on the other hand, establish causal links but these might be arbitrary. This means that a combination of the two is the most effective design. Each makes up for the weakness of the other.

CHAPTER 3

Longitudinal Study Methods

We had decided to do both a longitudinal and a training study and to do them at the same time. We wanted to find out whether the rhyming skills children develop before they go to school could be related to their progress in reading, and also whether training rhyming skills would noticeably improve reading levels. We turn first to the longitudinal measures. We wanted to know whether a child's ability to spot rhyme and alliteration before he begins to read is related to his subsequent success with learning to read and to write. This meant several things.

One point was that we needed to see a lot of children. Any longitudinal study of reading demands large numbers because reading and writing are skills that clearly are influenced by a number of things. You can only hope to sort out the different influences when you have reasonable numbers in your study. Another thing that we had to think about, of course, was making sure that our children were a reasonable cross section of children as a whole, and this meant seeing them in several different neighborhoods.

A second point we had to consider was the range of tests. Obviously we were going to test how well the children could detect rhyme and alliteration. But we had to use other measures as well. Here we had to be careful about two things. One was the nature of our rhyming and alliteration tests. These, as will be seen, involved memory, so we had to test how much the children remembered of the words in these tests in order to be sure that the relationships between rhyming and reading could not be explained away as the product of differences in memory.

But we also had to think of other more global influences. Suppose that we looked only at the relation between their scores on tests of rhyme and alliteration to their progress in reading. Suppose too that we showed that the more skilled children were with rhymes the faster they learned to read and write. On its own this result would be completely ambiguous; it could be explained in terms of other, easily measured, influences such as intelligence and verbal ability. It could simply be the case that brighter children rhyme better and also learn to read faster because of their greater intelligence. So we had to include measures of intelligence and of verbal ability to make sure that there were links between rhyming skills and reading that were independent of these other influences.

We also had to worry about our educational measures. Obviously we had to find out how well children did in reading and spelling, because that was what our hypothesis was about. But there was a danger here too, simply because this hypothesis was so specific to reading and spelling. It would have been wrong to look only at reading and spelling, because in that case we could be measuring some general educational skill and not something particular to reading and spelling. After all, our hypothesis was that early experiences with rhyming and alliteration help a child to break up words into phonological segments and to group words on the basis of these segments, and that this in turn helps him to conquer the alphabetic code and to learn how to read and write. If this hypothesis is right, rhyming and alliteration should have no direct effect on other skills the child has to learn at school such as learning about number. This would mean that rhyming should be linked a great deal more closely to learning how to read than to learning how to do sums. Obviously we had to check this point, which meant that we had to include mathematical tests as well.

Let us turn now to our attempts to take care of all these points.

The Children in the Project

All in all 403 children took part in our project. They were either four or five years old when we first saw them and when the project ended they were eight or nine. But behind these bald figures there are several other stories to be told.

One is that we actually tested 503 children at the start but rejected 100 of them who showed some signs of already being able to read at the start of the project. We reasoned that we should test children on rhyming and alliteration before they had begun to make any progress in reading. That argument of course ruled out children who could already read at the time of the initial tests. What we did at that time was to give all the children a reading test (the Schonell reading test) and rule out all those children who read any words in it at all.

A second point to be made is that our sample should be divided into two groups: a group we called the Nursery Group in which the children were four years old when we first saw them, and a Primary Group whose children were five years old at that time.

The distinction is an important one for two reasons. One is that the younger children were at nursery school and the older ones at primary school when we first saw them. In Britain rather less than half the children go to nursery school; all, by law, have to go to primary school when they reach the age of five.

The second reason for separating the two groups is even more important. We found that we had, when we saw the children first, to give the two age groups different tests of sensitivity to rhyme and alliteration. The ages of the two groups differed by an average of only six months, but even so the test that we gave the four year olds was too easy for their elders, and the test that was right for the five year olds was usually impossibly difficult for the younger children.

A final point is an obvious one. Though we started the project with 403 children we ended it with fewer. In fact we were quite pleased with the small number of dropouts. We knew that we were bound to lose some children over the four-year period, but in the end only 35 did drop out, leaving us with a final number of 368 children. Many of the remaining 368 children did change schools, but the moves were local ones. This contained dispersion made our job rather a hard one, for the children who remained in our sample till the end of the project were spread around forty-three schools, some of which were, from our point of view, quite far-flung.

All of the figures which we shall present concern the 368 children who remained in the project from start to finish, of which 104 were in the Nursery Group, and 264 in the Primary Group. The ages of the children in the two groups and their English Picture Vocabulary Test (E.P.V.T.) scores are given in table 4. The E.P.V.T. is a British version of the Peabody Picture Vocabulary Test (P.P.V.T.). The two are very alike except that the E.P.V.T. is standardized in Britain and excludes the few essentially un-British objects (such as a hydrant) that feature in the P.P.V.T. The table shows that the children in both groups represented a wide range of abilities. Their average E.P.V.T. score was some way above the mean for the population, which suggests that on the whole our sample was above the average intellectual level for children of that age: this suggestion, however, must be treated with some caution since the E.P.V.T. is a test of vocabulary and not a general test of intelligence.

TABLE 4. English Picture Vocabulary Test (E.P.V.T.) Scores for the Nursery and Primary Groups at the Time of the Initial Tests

	Nursery Group ($N = 104$)	Primary Group ($N = 264$)	Whole Sample ($N = 368$)
Mean Age	4y 11m	5y 6m	5y 4m
Mean E.P.V.T.	110.63	109.39	109.74
Standard deviation	11.95	11.55	11.66
Range	81–139	90–140	81–140

The Tests

Initial Tests

We shall confine ourselves to the main tests. We did give several others, but we shall have to write about them some- where else.

The Tests of Sound Categorization

These, from our point of view, were the most important. (Most of the others we shall be describing are simply there to make sure that the relationship between sound categorization and reading cannot be explained in terms of some other mea- surable ability.)

"Sound categorization" is the term that we use for detecting alliteration and rhyme. Our way of measuring it was very nearly exactly the same as in the rhyming and alliteration ex- periment comparing backward and normal readers described in the first chapter. Once again we used an "oddity" measure. We said either three or four words at a time, and all the words but one shared a common sound. The child's task was to spot the odd word out. The procedure was entirely verbal.

Each child was seen individually. He was asked if he could recite any nursery rhymes. Then the experimenter suggested a rhyme and encouraged the child to produce the rhyming words.

Do you know Hickory dickory dock?
Hickory dickory dock, The mouse ran up the . . . ?
Yes. Clock. Clock/dock. They sound alike, don't they?
Do you know Jack and Jill?
Jack and Jill, Went up the . . . ?
Yes. Hill. Jill/hill. Tell me another word that sounds like hill.

Experimenter (E):   pill
Child (C):   . . .

E: will
C: . . .

The experimenter and the child produced rhyming words
alternately, until the experimenter introduced a word that was
blatantly incorrect. If there was no quick negative response
from the child the error was pointed out. For example:

E: hat
C: . . .
E: rat
C: . . .
E: table
C: . . .
E: That doesn't sound right, does it?

The word game continued until the child realized that he
had to say when a word was incorrect. We then said,

Now I am going to say four words, and I want you to tell
me which word is the odd one out [or doesn't go]. Wait
until I have said all the words before you tell me which one
it is. Cat, hat, man, fat.

We simply spoke the three or four words on every trial, and
the child told us which of them he thought to be the odd one.
We always explained that the odd word would be in a different
position each time so that the game would not be too easy.
(The full test procedure is explained in Bradley 1980.)

Before a different condition was introduced we would say,
"This next lot is a bit different. Let us have a practice first." If
the new condition was the first sound condition, we would
begin by playing a game of "I spy." Once again we would
introduce an inappropriate word into the game and encourage
the child to spot the odd word, for example,

E: I spy with my little eye something beginning with *p*
C: pin

E: paper
C: pencil
E: window

After several games we would begin the new trials, but we would again explain that the odd word would be in a different position each time to make the game more difficult.

Here we come to the difference between the two age groups. We found it best to give the younger children only three words at a time; four words seemed to tax their memory too much and to lead to uniformly low performance. On the other hand three words seemed rather easy for the five year olds, whereas four seemed, nicely, not too easy and not too hard for them.

Apart from this, the procedure was exactly the same for the two groups. Each child went through thirty sound categorization trials, and these were divided into three conditions with ten trials each. These conditions were First Sound, Middle Sound, and End Sound. The difference among them was in the position of the sound that three out of the four words had in common and the odd word out did not share. Table 5 shows how this was done. The table gives all the words given to both age groups in their thirty-trial test of sound categorization. These, it can be seen, are genuinely phonological tasks. The child can only solve them by realizing that all but one of the words in each set shares a common phonological segment, and that this segment is not to be found in the odd word out.

Memory
Our oddity tasks involve memory as well as phonological skills. The child must remember the three or four words if he is to say which is the odd one out. So we felt that we had to look at how well they could remember the words they were given in the sound categorization tests.

In a separate test we gave the children exactly the same sets of words, trial by trial, as they were given in the sound cate-

TABLE 5. Words Given in the Initial Sound Categorization Test

Five-Year-Old Children (Primary Group)

First Sound				End Sound				Middle Sound			
Practice				Practice				Practice			
rot	rod	rock	*box*	*fan*	cat	hat	mat	mop	hop	*tap*	lop
lick	lid	*miss*	lip	leg	peg	hen	*beg*	pat	bat	*fit*	cat
Test				Test				Test			
bud	bun	bus	*rug*	pin	win	*sit*	fin	lot	cot	pot	*hat*
pip	pin	*hill*	pig	*doll*	hop	top	pop	fun	*pin*	bun	gun
ham	*tap*	had	hat	bun	*hut*	gun	sun	*hug*	dig	pig	wig
peg	pen	*well*	pet	map	cap	gap	*pal*	red	fed	*lid*	bed
kid	kick	kiss	*fill*	*men*	red	bed	fed	wag	rag	bag	*leg*
lot	*mop*	lock	log	wig	fig	*pin*	dig	fell	*doll*	well	bell
leap	mean	meal	meat	weed	*peel*	need	deed	*man*	bin	pin	tin
crack	crab	crag	*trap*	pack	lack	*sad*	back	fog	dog	*mug*	log
slim	*flip*	slick	slip	sand	hand	land	*bank*	feed	need	*wood*	seed
roof	room	*food*	root	sink	*mint*	pink	wink	fish	dish	wish	*mash*

Four-Year-Old Children (Nursery Group)

First Sound			End Sound			Middle Sound		
Practice			Practice			Practice		
lid	lip	*miss*	*fan*	cat	hat	hop	top	*sap*
cat	man	map	leg	peg	*hen*	*pet*	nut	cut
Test			Test			Test		
hill	pig	pin	pin	win	*sit*	cop	pot	*hut*
bus	bun	*rug*	*doll*	hop	top	*pin*	bun	gun
tap	hat	ham	bun	gun	*hut*	pig	wig	hug
cup	cut	*fun*	*pal*	map	cap	*lid*	bed	head
net	neck	*bed*	*men*	head	bed	*leg*	bag	rag
pot	dog	doll	*pin*	wig	fig	bell	well	*doll*
lad	jam	jack	rod	nod	*sock*	*man*	tin	pin
fill	kick	kiss	*sun*	bud	mud	dog	log	*mug*
wet	web	*bell*	nut	cut	*fun*	*lip*	cup	pup
log	lock	*mop*	well	bell	*pet*	bat	cat	*fit*

gorization tests. This time, however, the child had to repeat the words back to us straightaway. This thirty-trial test of memory measured in as direct a way as possible the child's ability to remember the words he was given in the sound categorization tests.

E.P.V.T.

We felt that it was absolutely necessary to get an immediate measure of the children's vocabulary as well, in order to show that our sound categorization tests were more than mere measures of verbal skills, and that they were related to progress in reading quite independently of the children's language. All the children, therefore, were given the E.P.V.T., a picture vocabulary test, in which the children are shown four pictures at a time and are asked each time to identify the one picture that the tester names. As we noted before this is the British version of the P.P.V.T. We have already presented the mean E.P.V.T. scores in table 4.

Other Tests

At the same time we gave all the children several other tests including tests of drawing and of rhythm, as well as other measures of memory. We also gathered data about the majority of the children in our sample from a checklist which teachers in local schools fill in about each child shortly after he or she arrives at school and also two years later. However, we will not have the space to describe these other measures in this monograph.

Final Tests

The project lasted about four years. In fact the time between our seeing the first child (March, 1978) and gathering the last bit of data (May, 1982) was a little over four years. But the average time between first giving a child our sound categorization tests and testing the same child's reading and spelling skills at the end of the project was much less than this. The mean age of the children when first tested was five years, four months. It was eight years, four months at the final tests of reading and spelling, making the average gap between those two events three years.

Since our main concern was how well our initial measures predicted the children's success in reading and spelling, our chief outcome measures were standardized tests of reading and spelling. We did take some intervening measures of these skills, but in this monograph we shall be dealing only with the final reading and spelling scores. In other words we shall be asking how well a child's sound categorization skills predict his progress in reading and spelling three and a half years later, and predict them independently of extraneous variables such as intelligence and verbal skills.

The Neale Analysis of Reading
All 368 children were given the Neale analysis of reading in the last six months of the project. This is a well-known standardized test in which children have to read graded prose passages aloud and then are asked questions about the passages' meaning. It yields three scores: accuracy, comprehension, and speed. When we calculated the Neale reading ages that we analyze in this monograph, we took the traditional step of looking at the accuracy and comprehension scores and taking the lower of the two. That figure gave us the Neale reading age.

The Schonell Test of Reading
At the same time we gave a single word reading test, the Schonell (Schonell and Goodacre 1971). The children simply had to read a graded series of words one at a time and were scored right or wrong on each word.

The Schonell Test of Spelling
We needed a test of spelling and we chose the Schonell (Schonell 1950). In this test a series of words, again graded, is read to the child who has to write each one out as soon as he hears it.

Wechsler Intelligence Scale for Children (W.I.S.C.)
For the reasons just given, we felt that we had to include a measure of intelligence. We chose the W.I.S.C., partly because we think that it is a good test and partly because many of the major studies of backwardness in reading have also used it. We wanted to see how our results compared to theirs.

Not having the resources to give each of the 368 children the full W.I.S.C., we had to be content with a shorter version. We decided to use the four tests that traditionally make up the short form of the W.I.S.C. (Maxwell 1959): these are (Verbal) Similarities and Vocabulary, and (Performance) Object Assembly and Block Design. But we decided to add one more verbal and one more performance test. These were Digit Span (Verbal) and Coding (Performance). We added these last subtests because there is consistent evidence that they are particularly difficult for children with reading difficulties and we felt that it would be useful to know about the relations between them and our measures of sound categorization (Naidoo 1972).

We did manage to give the full version of the W.I.S.C. to all the children (experimental and control groups) in the training study. We felt that we needed detailed information about them. (The W.I.S.C. had been very recently revised at the time of the study and was referred to as the W.I.S.C./R. during the changeover period.)

Table 6 shows the I.Q. figures, calculated from these subtests, for the two groups and for the sample as a whole. These figures confirm the suggestion gleaned from the E.P.V.T.

TABLE 6. W.I.S.C. (short form) I.Q. Scores for the Nursery and Primary Groups at the Time of the Final Tests

	Nursery Group ($N = 104$)	Primary Group ($N = 264$)	Whole Sample ($N = 368$)
Mean age	8y 4m	8y 3m	8y 4m
Mean I.Q.	113.39	106.79	108.65
Standard deviation	15.82	16.92	16.86
Range	76–145	51–151	51–151

scores that on average our sample was above normal in intellectual ability. The W.I.S.C. figures also confirm that our sample covered a wide range of abilities.

Sound Categorization
Our main concern was with the relation between the initial sound categorization scores and reading and spelling three and a half years later. But we decided that we should find out how well each child could handle the tests of sound categorization at the end, as well as at the beginning, of the project. We thought that it was important to know whether the relation between sound categorization and reading and spelling stayed constant as children make progress in reading.

We gave each child the same tests of sound categorization as were given to the five-year-old children at the beginning. We gave the children the same words in exactly the same way as before. We also tested their memory for these words in the same way as before.

The N.F.E.R. Test of Mathematical Skills
At the end of the project we gave as many children as possible (the number in the end was 263 of whom 69 came from the nursery group and 194 from the primary group) a test of mathematical skills. This is a group test devised by the National Foundation for Educational Research (N.F.E.R.) and standardized on British children (N.F.E.R. 1970). It is designed for children aged between seven years, six months and eight years, six months. The test yields a ratio score, the average for any age being one hundred.

Summary

We started with a group of 403 children. By the end of our project that number stood at 368. Of these 368, 104 were four year olds and at nursery school when we first saw them, while 268 were five year olds and had just started primary school at the time of these first tests.

The most important of our initial tests were the tests of sound categorization. In these tests the children heard three or four words per trial and had to judge each time which of the words was the odd one out, i.e., did not possess a sound common to the other words.

At the same time we tested the children's ability to remember these words, and we also took a measure of their verbal ability (E.P.V.T.).

We related these initial scores to our final scores that were taken on average three years later. In the final tests we took two measures of reading, and one of spelling. We also tested the children's intelligence.

CHAPTER 4

The Total Sound
Categorization Scores

The main question in this chapter is whether the children's skill at categorizing words by their sound when they were four and five years old predicted their reading and spelling skills three and a half years later at the age of eight or more. We will start with a brief description of the children and of their initial and final scores, and then continue with an analysis of the relationship between these two sets of scores.

The Children

We will confine our description to the 368 children who completed the project. These 368 were divided into two groups, those who were four years old and at nursery school at the beginning of the project, and those who were, at that time, five years old and in primary schools. The Nursery Group consisted of 104, the Primary Group of 264, children.

We need to know how representative these children were. As we saw in chapter 3, our children overall were rather above average ability. But their E.P.V.T. and W.I.S.C. scores demonstrated that our sample represented a wide range of abilities.

Initial Scores in Sound Categorization

Table 7 shows the mean scores of each group in the sound categorization tests given at the beginning of the project. Scores represent the number of correct answers out of ten trials in each of the three conditions (First Sound, Middle

Sound, and End Sound) as explained in chapter 3. A total score for all thirty trials is also given.

Since three words were given on each trial to the Nursery Group and four words to the Primary Group, the children in the former group could produce a score of 3.3 if they were simply acting randomly: in the second group random responses would lead to a score of 2.5. Anything above these scores is therefore above chance level and it can be seen that on the whole the children's scores were well above that. So we think that we have confirmed our hypothesis that children are aware of phonological categories before they learn to read. Ours is easily the largest and most systematic study to date to demonstrate that children do understand a great deal about the sound properties of their language before they learn to read.

These tasks were by no means too easy. We found a range of scores. Some children made hardly any mistakes, others a great deal, and most lay somewhere between. This was encouraging because we needed a range to have any chance of relating these scores to success in reading.

TABLE 7.   Initial Scores in Sound Categorization

	Nursery Group (N = 104)	Primary Group (N = 264)
Age	4y 11m	5y 6m
First Sound		
Mean (out of 10)	5.69	5.34
Standard deviation	1.90	2.30
Middle Sound		
Mean (out of 10)	7.53	6.89
Standard deviation	1.96	2.35
End Sound		
Mean (out of 10)	7.42	6.67
Standard deviation	2.09	2.33
Total Scores		
Mean (out of 30)	20.68	18.90
Standard deviation	4.92	5.90

We can turn to the pattern of scores in the three conditions. The table shows very clearly that rhyming, tested by the Middle Sound and End Sound conditions, is much easier than alliteration, which is tested by the First Sound condition. Though both groups are above chance in the First Sound condition, the alliterative condition, it still is a particularly difficult one for them. This is an interesting result, and one which we cannot explain with any confidence. It may be due simply to experience: young children probably are exposed to rhymes more than to alliteration. We do however have other, independent evidence of a developmental difference between rhyme and alliteration. In a study of children aged between four and six years (Bradley 1982) it emerged that children recognize rhyme some time before alliteration, and that recognition of alliteration only seems to get under way after children go to school.

Final Educational Scores

Table 8 gives the final scores in the tests of reading, spelling, and mathematics three years later when the children were eight years old or more. Once again our measures tapped a wide range of ability. But there is a clear difference between

TABLE 8.   Final Scores for Reading and Spelling, in Months

	Nursery Group	Primary Group	Whole Sample
Mean age	101.85	101.42	101.54
Standard deviation	2.24	4.77	4.21
Mean Neale reading age	105.13	101.30	102.38
Standard deviation	16.20	15.82	16.00
Mean Schonell reading age	103.13	100.03	100.91
Standard deviation	15.58	16.99	16.64
Mean Schonell spelling age	97.27	93.94	94.88
Standard deviation	17.62	17.51	17.58

these scores and our W.I.S.C. and E.P.V.T. results. Although these latter tests showed that our group overall were above average in intellectual and verbal skills, their reading ages were very close to their chronological ages. They read no better than average and indeed spelled rather worse than the average for the population at large even though their aptitude scores were above normal.

It is exactly the same story with the mathematics scores, as table 9 shows. The test we gave was standardized (a score of 100 is the average for the population). The 264 children to whom we gave the test had I.Q.'s that were above average, but their mathematical scores were slightly below average.

We have no ready explanation for this general pattern of higher than normal aptitude scores combined with either normal or rather lower than normal achievement scores. But we were pleased, when we turned to the relation between our initial and final scores, that the average reading, spelling, and mathematical scores of our group had turned out to be around the average for the normal population.

Relations between the Initial Scores and the Final Scores

Each child was given a total score for sound categorization—his score for all three conditions combined. This was then related to the child's reading, spelling, and mathematical levels at the end of the project. Table 10 gives the simple correlations of

TABLE 9.   Final Scores in Mathematics (M.A.T.B.)

	Nursery Group (N = 69)	Primary Group (N = 195)
Mean M.A.T.B.	99.71	94.22
Standard deviation	15.78	12.21
Mean I.Q.	113.99	107.94
Standard deviation	15.55	16.48

the final reading, spelling, and mathematical scores with the initial sound categorization scores, the initial E.P.V.T. scores, and I.Q.

It can easily be seen that the correlations between sound categorization and reading and spelling several years later are high. They are at least as high as, and often higher than, the relationship between our aptitude measures (E.P.V.T. and W.I.S.C.) and reading and spelling, and this seems to us to be particularly striking in the case of the W.I.S.C.; after all, the sound categorization tests were given three years before the final reading scores were gathered, whereas the W.I.S.C. and reading tests were administered at the same time.

However, simple correlations on their own are not enough. Part of the reason for the high correlation between sound categorization and reading and spelling may be that intelligent children who are good at sound categorization also learn to read well. We need to know about the influence of sound categorization on its own and quite apart from other influences such as intelligence or verbal skill or memory. For this we have to turn to multiple regressions.

We wanted to know whether sound categorization predicted

TABLE 10.   Simple Correlations between Initial and Final Scores

Initial Scores	Final Scores			
	Neale Reading	Schonell Reading	Schonell Spelling	Math
Nursery Group				
Total sound				
categorization	.52	.57	.48	.33
E.P.V.T.	.52	.51	.33	.42
W.I.S.C.	.45	.40	.36	.55
Primary Group				
Total sound				
categorization	.47	.45	.44	.45
E.P.V.T.	.44	.39	.33	.42
W.I.S.C.	.47	.44	.37	.57

reading and spelling three and a half years later *when the influences of vocabulary, intelligence, and the child's ability to remember the words which he had to categorize at the beginning of the project had been removed.* Multiple regression is an excellent way of finding this sort of thing out. There are various ways of doing multiple regressions, but for our purposes the only appropriate way, as well as the toughest way, was to devise multiple regressions in which the steps were entered in a fixed order. We entered our variables in the same predetermined order, always leaving sound categorization, the variable that interested us most, till last.

This may sound complex to those readers who are not familiar with the technique, but in fact the rationale behind a fixed order multiple regression can be explained very quickly. You have an outcome measure like reading—the dependent variable—and another variable, in our case sound categorization, which you want to relate to that outcome measure: but you also have a host of other variables that are probably related to reading too and you want to remove the effects of these.

In our case these other variables were (1) the child's age when he was given the final tests of reading and spelling, (2) the child's E.P.V.T. score at that time, (3) the child's I.Q., and (4) the child's ability to recall the words in the initial sound categorization tests. It can easily be seen that all four of these variables could be related both to sound categorization and to reading. Obviously the children's age at the time when their reading and spelling levels (which are expressed in reading and spelling ages) were measured could have been a potent influence on these levels. Obviously, too, a child's intelligence or his verbal skills could affect sound categorization and reading as well, and so we must take steps to remove their influence. The fourth variable, recall, must also be controlled: our sound categorization tests involved memory, because the child had to remember the words in our sound categorization tests in order to categorize them, and memory must also play a role in learning to read. So, we felt we could only talk about the relationships between sound categorization and reading/spelling after the effects of these four factors had been eliminated.

In our multiple regressions, we entered first the child's age at the time of the reading and spelling tests. This told us how much of the variance in reading and spelling (which is measured in reading/spelling age) could be explained in terms of how old the child was then. Next we entered E.P.V.T. and found out how much of the variance in reading or spelling was due to the child's verbal skills after the variance due to age had been removed. Next we entered I.Q. and saw how much variance in the dependent variable could be explained in terms of the children's intelligence after the influence of age and E.P.V.T. had been removed, and so on. Thus when we took the next and final step of entering the sound categorization scores we were in a position to find out how much of the variance in reading and spelling was due to sound categorization independent of age, verbal skill, intelligence, and memory.

Table 11 gives the first of these multiple regressions. In this the outcome measure was the nursery group's reading levels at the end of the project as assessed by the Neale reading test. For the reasons just given the five steps in the multiple regression were, in order, (1) age, (2) E.P.V.T., (3) W.I.S.C., (4) memory, and (5) *the total sound categorization scores for each child.* It is as well to note now that for the rest of this chapter we shall be dealing with these total sound categoriza-

TABLE 11.   Stepwise Multiple Regressions for Nursery Group; Dependent Variable, Neale Reading Age

Step		Additional Variance[a]
1	Chronological age	0.61%
2	E.P.V.T.	26.51
3	W.I.S.C.	8.24
4	Memory	5.95
5	Sound categorization	6.24

[a]Significance of contribution of sound categorization: $F = 11.7$, df 1,98, $p < .001$

tion scores, by which we mean the score reached for each child by adding together his score for all three sound categorization conditions (First, Middle, and End Sounds).

The most obviously striking thing about this table is that the children's verbal skills (E.P.V.T.) and intelligence (W.I.S.C.) account for the lion's share of the variance in the children's eventual reading levels. But this is not at all surprising. One would expect that a child's intelligence and his adeptness with language would have a pronounced effect on his progress in learning to read and to spell.

In contrast, at first sight the amount of variance accounted for by the children's sound categorization scores looks rather modest—only 6.24 percent. But it has to be remembered that this variance is what remains after the powerful influence of verbal ability and intelligence has been removed. In other words this 6.24 percent figure represents the influence of sound categorization once verbal ability, intelligence, age, and memory have been controlled. Looked at in this way it is clear that such a relationship is quite impressive, and this is reflected by its high significance level. The multiple regression demonstrates that there is a significant relationship between sound categorization and reading over and above, and quite independently from, the obvious influences of intelligence and verbal ability.

We can now turn to the equivalent scores in the Primary Group, which are given in table 12. Here the pattern is very similar. Again the lion's share of the variance is taken up by

TABLE 12.   Stepwise Multiple Regressions for Primary Group; Dependent Variable, Neale Reading Age

Step		Additional Variance[a]
1	Chronological age	0.87%
2	E.P.V.T.	20.10
3	W.I.S.C.	8.96
4	Memory	0.03
5	Sound categorization	4.56

[a]Significance of contribution of sound categorization: $F = 17.92$, df 1,258, $p < .001$

the two aptitude tests (E.P.V.T. and W.I.S.C.) while the additional variance left over is modest and indeed rather smaller than in the case of the nursery group. But it is highly significant, and again one must note that it happens even after the effects of intelligence and verbal ability have been completely controlled.

Thus both multiple regressions in which Neale reading levels were the outcome measure demonstrate that sound categorization does have a strong and significant relationship to children's progress in reading even after as long a period as three years. Here is our first evidence that a child's skill at categorizing sounds before he learns to read will affect his progress in reading as long as three years later.

Is this true of the other outcome measures? Tables 13 and 14 give the figures for the two groups when the outcome mea-

TABLE 13. Stepwise Multiple Regressions for Nursery Group; Dependent Variable, Schonell Reading Age

Step		Additional Variance[a]
1	Chronological age	0.01%
2	E.P.V.T.	26.27
3	W.I.S.C.	5.11
4	Memory	5.93
5	Sound categorization	9.84

[a]Significance of contribution of sound categorization: $F = 18.5$, df 1,98, $p < .001$

TABLE 14. Stepwise Multiple Regressions for Primary Group; Dependent Variable, Schonell Reading Age

Step		Additional Variance[a]
1	Chronological age	1.32%
2	E.P.V.T.	16.18
3	W.I.S.C.	8.32
4	Memory	0.00
5	Sound categorization	4.06

[a]Significance of contribution of sound categorization: $F = 14.94$, df 1,258, $p < .001$

sure was the children's reading levels as measured by the
Schonell reading test.

Here the amount of variation in the nursery group's reading
levels that can be traced back to the children's sound categorization skills three years earlier is actually higher than it was
when Neale reading levels were considered—9.84 percent as
opposed to 6.24 percent. So it is not surprising that again there
was a highly significant relationship between the initial sound
categorization scores and the children's eventual reading levels. It is worth repeating that this relationship is entirely independent of the children's intelligence and verbal skills.

In the primary group this relationship was somewhat
smaller, but it was still highly significant. Table 14 certainly
shows that the amount of variance that can be explained as the
product of the children's initial sound categorization skills is
only 4.06 percent. But in this particular case the overall proportion of the variance that could be accounted for by all five
variables together was rather low. We were not sure why this
was so, but we noted that once again there was a highly significant relationship between the initial sound categorization
scores and reading level three years later.

All four multiple regressions that tracked the relationship
between the total initial sound categorization scores and reading demonstrated the same significant relationship. We have
therefore established that a child's preschool skill at taking
apart and categorizing the sounds in words is definitely connected to his eventual progress in learning to read, and that
the connection is quite independent of intelligence and linguistic skill. Moreover this connection spans three years and
applies to a large number of children with a wide range of
backgrounds and skills. We consider this to be an important
discovery.

Now we can turn to spelling. Table 15 gives the multiple
regression of the nursery group's spelling levels. Here again a
highly significant relationship is evident. Once again the children's initial sound categorization scores are strongly con-

nected to their progress over three years: this time the progress is in spelling.

Table 16 tells much the same story with the primary group's spelling levels. This, the sixth of our multiple regressions involving the children's total sound categorization scores, comes to much the same conclusion as the others. For the sixth time we found a highly significant relationship between these scores and our outcome measure—in this case spelling—three years later.

The picture is so clear and so consistent that it hardly needs a comment. We need only say that as far as the total sound categorization scores are concerned our results are positive. We have established a definite connection between the two things which interest us most, sound categorization and learning to read and write.

TABLE 15.   Stepwise Multiple Regressions for Nursery Group; Dependent Variable, Schonell Spelling Age

Step		Additional Variance[a]
1	Chronological age	1.88%
2	E.P.V.T.	9.99
3	W.I.S.C.	7.79
4	Memory	5.84
5	Sound categorization	8.10

[a]Significance of contribution of sound categorization: $F = 11.94$, df 1,98, $p < .001$

TABLE 16.   Stepwise Multiple Regressions for Primary Group; Dependent Variable, Schonell Spelling Age

Step		Additional Variance[a]
1	Chronological age	1.77%
2	E.P.V.T.	10.57
3	W.I.S.C.	6.84
4	Memory	0.02
5	Sound categorization	5.59

[a]Significance of contribution of sound categorization: $F = 19.15$, df 1,98, $p < .001$

One major question, however, remains. It is our hypothesis not only that the connection exists, but also that it is a specific one. By this we mean that a child's sound categorization skills will have a particular effect on reading and spelling, and not on educational achievement in general. This was why we included a test of mathematical achievement. Having predicted that the sound categorization scores would not be connected to mathematics as they are to reading and spelling, we carried out the same kind of multiple regressions with mathematics as the outcome measure as we had with reading and spelling.

Before describing these regressions we need to make two points. One is a reminder that the numbers of children taking the mathematics test were somewhat smaller—69 in the Nursery Group and 195 in the Primary Group. The second—a minor detail—is that we did not need to enter age in these regressions because the mathematics score is a ratio score that takes the child's age into account. So we had four rather than five steps in these multiple regressions.

Table 17 shows the analysis of the Nursery Group's scores. This table provides a very sharp contrast with the earlier results. Very little of the variance of the children's mathematics scores can be attributed to their sound categorization skills. The connection comes nowhere near statistical significance. We have to conclude that there was no relationship between these children's skills with sound categories and their mathematical abilities three years later.

TABLE 17.   Stepwise Multiple Regressions for Nursery Group; Dependent Variable, Mathematics Scores

Step		Additional Variance[a]
1	E.P.V.T.	17.80%
2	W.I.S.C.	16.03
3	Memory	4.15
4	Sound categorization	1.36

[a]Significance of contribution of sound categorization: $F = 1.44$, df 1,65, p = not significant

This is an interesting and pleasing result. It certainly supports our hypothesis of a specific connection between sound categorization and learning to read and write. In the nursery group at least there does seem to be a connection between these two things and not between sound categorization and mathematics.

We must now look to see whether the same specific connection can be found in the primary group. Table 18 gives the multiple regression of their mathematical levels, and it paints a very different picture. There is a surprising result in this table. The amount of variance in mathematical levels accounted for by sound categorization is not particularly high—3.89 percent—but it is highly significant.

Here, it seems, is our first negative result. We had predicted no relationship between sound categorization and mathematics. We found none in the Nursery Group. But now we find that a relationship does exist in the Primary Group. Of this group we cannot at the moment say that the connection between sound categorization and learning to read and write is a specific one: here sound categorization touches mathematics as well.

At first sight this seems a disappointment. But it presents an interesting puzzle too. Why, we must ask, is there this sharp difference between the two groups? What is the reason for the unexpected connection between sound categorization and math in the Primary Group? There seems no particular reason why a child's facility at categorizing sounds should have any bearing whatsoever on his success in learning how to do sums.

TABLE 18. Stepwise Multiple Regressions for Primary Group; Dependent Variable, Mathematics Scores

Step		Additional Variance[a]
1	E.P.V.T.	17.47%
2	W.I.S.C.	16.65
3	Memory	0.97
4	Sound categorization	3.89

[a]Significance of contribution of sound categorization: $F = 12.10$, df 1,190, $p < .001$

The scores we have considered so far—the total sound categorization scores—offer no solution. But we have yet to consider the three sound categorization conditions separately, and they provide an interesting explanation for this apparent anomaly. As we shall see in the next chapter, it turns out not to be an anomaly at all.

The eight multiple regressions can be summarized quite simply. The Nursery Group's results present a copybook picture. Their initial sound categorization scores are related to reading and spelling three years later, but not to mathematics. The Primary Group is less straightforward. These children's sound categorization scores are related to all three educational skills: reading, spelling, and mathematics. We can be sure of a specific connection in the Nursery Group. With the Primary Group we must suspend judgment until we have looked at the further analyses which are presented in the next chapter.

Summary

Our measures of sound categorization do show that children are, though to varying degrees, aware of the segments of sound in words before they begin to read or write.

Our large sample covered a considerable range in intellectual ability and in educational achievement as well as in sound categorization skills.

These sound categorization skills were consistently related to reading and spelling levels three years later, and this relationship existed even when the influence of intelligence and linguistic ability had been removed.

The connection between the initial skills and reading and writing was specific in the case of the Nursery Group since there was no significant connection in this group's scores between sound categorization and mathematics. However, in the Primary Group the connection was not specific: sound categorization predicted mathematical levels as well as reading and spelling. We shall deal with this difference in the next chapter.

CHAPTER 5

The Different Sound Conditions

The sound categorization scores that we have analyzed so far have been the children's total scores. These total scores give us a useful picture of each child's overall ability to take words apart and to see the connections between different words. But we cannot assume that the three different conditions that make up these total scores went the same way for each child. We already know that one of the conditions—the First Sound condition—was more difficult than the other two. Alliteration, in other words, was more difficult than rhyme. One implication of this difference is that it is possible that the different conditions might have been tapping different abilities.

Naturally we also analyzed these three conditions separately, and looked at their relations to the children's reading, spelling, and mathematical levels at the end of the project. We asked exactly the same questions and used exactly the same procedures to answer them as we had with the total sound categorization scores. We wanted to know whether the scores in each sound categorization condition were related to the children's progress in learning how to read and write. We also wanted to see whether the connection between each sound condition and reading and spelling was a specific one.

In fact this question of specificity loomed very large for us at the time that we turned to the scores for the three different sound conditions. We hoped that they might help us clear up the puzzle about the relation that we found in the Primary Group between the children's total sound categorization scores and mathematics.

The Correlations

Let us look at the correlations first. Table 19 shows the relations among the three sound categorization conditions and the four educational tests. It shows an extremely interesting pattern, the most striking feature of which is a very marked difference between the Nursery and Primary Groups.

Once again there were consistently high correlations between the initial sound categorization scores and reading and spelling, and these were to be found in both groups. However, there were also differences among the three conditions and these actually went in opposite directions for the two age groups. In the Primary Group the condition which correlates most strongly with their eventual reading and spelling is the alliteration condition: it seems that their ability at five years of age to categorize a word by its first sound was the best indicator of their eventual success in learning to read and write. In

TABLE 19.   Simple Correlations between Initial Scores in Sound Categorization and Final Reading, Spelling, and Math Scores

Initial Scores	Final Scores			
	Neale Reading	Schonell Reading	Schonell Spelling	Mathematics
Nursery Group				
First Sound				
Condition	.38	.39	.32	.22
Middle Sound				
Condition	.45	.52	.42	.34
End Sound				
Condition	.47	.50	.45	.23
Primary Group				
First Sound				
Condition	.48	.43	.46	.52
Middle Sound				
Condition	.37	.37	.34	.30
End Sound				
Condition	.37	.33	.31	.32

fact it is more strongly related than the total sound categorization scores to these children's eventual reading and spelling levels.

It is quite a different story with the Nursery Group. The alliteration condition is actually the poorest indicator of their eventual success in reading and spelling. The best indicator is the End Sound condition, one of the two rhyming conditions.

With mathematics the two groups again diverge. Once again the relationships between initial sound categorization and final mathematical levels are stronger in the Primary than in the Nursery Group. But in the Primary Group this relationship concentrates in an extremely interesting way around one condition only, the alliteration condition. It seems that the original relationship in the Primary Group between total sound categorization scores and mathematics is mainly the product of the alliteration condition. That condition predicts all four educational tests extremely well. The other two conditions—Middle and End Sound—are related much more strongly to reading and spelling than to mathematics. The connection between the Middle and End Sound conditions is a specific one, while the connection between the alliteration condition and reading and spelling is not.

The picture is quite different in the case of the Nursery Group. There is no sign of any strong relation between any of the sound conditions and mathematics; the alliteration condition predicts their mathematical levels as poorly as do the other two sound conditions.

These correlations suggest an answer to the puzzle about the Primary Group's mathematical scores. The solution seems to lie in the difference between the alliteration condition and the other two sound conditions. For some reason the alliteration condition seems to predict educational progress in general, while the other two predict reading and spelling levels in particular. But simple correlations are not enough if we are to be sure that this is a genuine pattern. One cannot disentangle from these correlations how much of the educational variance was accounted for by the individual sound categorization scores. Multiple regressions do that.

Mathematics Scores

Let us reverse the sequence of the last chapter and turn first to the mathematics results, since these for the moment produce the greatest puzzle. Table 20 gives the results of three multiple regressions that deal with the Nursery Group's mathematical scores. These regressions took exactly the same form as those we described in chapter 4 except that in each case the last step in the fixed order of steps was always the scores for an individual sound condition. The three multiple regressions reported in table 20 shared the same first two steps (E.P.V.T. and W.I.S.C.) and differed only in their last two steps, the memory for the words in the particular condition being analyzed and the scores for the specific sound condition (First, Middle, or End Sound).

TABLE 20.   Multiple Regressions of the Three Sound Conditions for the Nursery Group; Dependent Variable, Mathematics Scores

Step	Additional Variance
All Regressions	
1 E.P.V.T.	17.80%
2 W.I.S.C.	16.02
First Sound[a]	
3 Memory for words	9.10%
4 Sound categorization	0.40
Middle Sound[b]	
3 Memory for words	2.73%
4 Sound categorization	3.02
End Sound[c]	
3 Memory for words	0.08%
4 Sound categorization	0.22

[a]Significance of contribution of sound categorization: $F = 0.45$, df 1,64, p = not significant

[b]Significance of contribution of sound categorization: $F = 3.19$, df 1,64, p = not significant

[c]Significance of contribution of sound categorization: $F = 0.21$, df 1,64, p = not significant

These multiple regressions show quite clearly that there is no significant link at all between any of the three sound conditions and mathematics in the Nursery Group. Once again we can conclude that for these children any link between sound categorization and reading is a specific one. It does not spread to mathematics.

This takes us to the Primary Group's mathematical scores. We need to know whether the ideas suggested by the simple correlations are right. Is it true that the alliteration condition produces the only significant relationship between sound categorization and mathematics? Table 21 shows that this is exactly the pattern.

Here indeed is a sharp division. The relation between the First Sound condition (alliteration) and mathematics is very strong and highly significant. Between the other two sound conditions and mathematics there is no significant connection at all. There is then a peculiar connection between alliteration

TABLE 21. Multiple Regressions of the Three Sound Conditions for the Primary Group; Dependent Variable, Mathematics Scores

Step	Additional Variance
All Regressions	
1 E.P.V.T.	17.31%
2 W.I.S.C.	17.02
First Sound[a]	
3 Memory for words	1.19%
4 Sound categorization	9.86
Middle Sound[b]	
3 Memory for words	0.36%
4 Sound categorization	1.15
End Sound[c]	
3 Memory for words	0.44%
4 Sound categorization	0.48

[a]Significance of contribution of sound categorization: $F = 34.11$, df 1,258, $p < .001$

[b]Significance of contribution of sound categorization: $F = 3.38$, df 1,190, $p =$ not significant

[c]Significance of contribution of sound categorization: $F = 1.39$, df 1,190, $p =$ not significant

as tested at five years and mathematics three years later. This connection demands an explanation and so does the fact that the relationship is only to be found in the Primary Group. But we are unlikely to be able to come up with a full explanation without first considering the multiple regressions which deal with reading and spelling.

The Nursery Group's Reading and Spelling Scores

Table 22 gives the three regressions which deal with the Nursery Group's reading levels, as assessed by the Neale. Here and in all the following tables the three regressions share the three first steps (age at the time of the final tests, E.P.V.T., and W.I.S.C.). There is very little to say about this table except that all three conditions were significantly related to the children's reading levels three years later. Let us stay with the

TABLE 22.   Multiple Regressions of the Three Sound Conditions for the Nursery Group; Dependent Variable, Neale Reading Age

Step	Additional Variance
All Regressions	
1 Chronological age	0.61%
2 E.P.V.T.	26.51
3 W.I.S.C.	8.24
First Sound[a]	
4 Memory for words	4.48%
5 Sound categorization	3.49
Middle Sound[b]	
4 Memory for words	4.99%
5 Sound categorization	4.10
End Sound[c]	
4 Memory for words	4.47%
5 Sound categorization	6.25

[a]Significance of contribution of first sound categorization: $F = 6.04$, df 1,98, $p < .025$
[b]Significance of contribution of middle sound categorization: $F = 7.23$, df 1,98, $p < .01$
[c]Significance of contribution of end sound categorization: $F = 11.35$, df 1,98, $p < .005$

Nursery Group and see whether the same pattern can be found with their Schonell scores.

Table 23 deals with the Schonell reading ages of the nursery group. Again all three sound conditions are related to the Nursery Group's final reading levels. We can now be sure that they do account for a significant part of the children's progress in learning to read.

Is this true too of the Nursery Group's final spelling levels? Table 24 shows that it is. The story of the connections between the Nursery Group's sound categorization scores and their educational progress over the next three years is now complete. It is a simple story and an interesting one. All measures of their skill at categorizing sounds, the three separate conditions separately and together, are related to reading and spelling to a significant degree. None is related to mathematical progress. In this group we have found an unambiguous and

TABLE 23. Multiple Regressions of the Three Sound Conditions for the Nursery Group; Dependent Variable, Schonell Reading Age

Step	Additional Variance
All Regressions	
1 Chronological age	0.84%
2 E.P.V.T.	26.27
3 W.I.S.C.	5.11
First Sound[a]	
4 Memory for words	3.72%
5 Sound categorization	3.96
Middle Sound[b]	
4 Memory for words	6.41%
5 Sound categorization	8.12
End Sound[c]	
4 Memory for words	4.13%
5 Sound categorization	8.90

[a]Significance of contribution of sound categorization: $F = 6.45$, df 1,98, $p < .025$

[b]Significance of contribution of sound categorization: $F = 14.95$, df 1,98, $p < .001$

[c]Significance of contribution of sound categorization: $F = 15.92$, df 1,98, $p < .001$

specific connection between knowing how to categorize words and later progress in learning to read and write. Our theory predicted this specific relationship. We have a good idea of its pathway from breaking up words into sound categories to coping with the segments of sound in words and the relationship of these segments to the alphabet to ultimate success in reading and spelling. The idea of this sequence is strongly supported by the Nursery Group's results. It was from our point of view a good group.

The Primary Group's Reading and Spelling Scores

What about the other group? We have already noted that the connection between sound categorization and mathematics in the Primary Group was sharply confined to the First Sound condition. But we must look first at the relationship of the

TABLE 24. Multiple Regressions of the Three Sound Conditions for the Nursery Group; Dependent Variable, Schonell Spelling Age

Step	Additional Variance
All Regressions	
1 Chronological age	1.88%
2 E.P.V.T.	9.99
3 W.I.S.C.	7.79
First Sound[a]	
4 Memory for words	4.64%
5 Sound categorization	3.65
Middle Sound[b]	
4 Memory for words	5.86%
5 Sound categorization	5.95
End Sound[c]	
4 Memory for words	3.38%
5 Sound categorization	8.05

[a]Significance of contribution of sound categorization: $F = 4.97$, df 1,98, $p < .05$
[b]Significance of contribution of sound categorization: $F = 8.50$, df 1,98, $p < .005$
[c]Significance of contribution of sound categorization: $F = 11.44$, df 1,98, $p < .005$

three conditions to this group's reading and spelling before we can begin to explain this very specific difference. Table 25 deals with this group's Neale reading scores. There is no problem here. There is a significant relationship between all three sound conditions and the children's eventual reading levels. The only other point to note is that the First Sound condition accounts for more variance and is more significantly related to Neale reading levels than are the other two conditions.

Table 26 gives the equivalent figures for the Schonell reading ages in the Primary Group. There is a slight shock in this table, which is that the End Sound condition is not related in any significant way to the children's Schonell reading levels. We are not entirely clear why this should be so. That condition was related to Neale reading levels. Otherwise the pattern is as before: in particular once again the First Sound condition was by far the best indicator of success in reading.

TABLE 25. Multiple Regressions of the Three Sound Conditions for the Primary Group; Dependent Variable, Neale Reading Age

Step	Additional Variance
All Regressions	
1 Chronological age	0.90%
2 E.P.V.T.	21.01
3 W.I.S.C.	8.49
First Sound[a]	
4 Memory for words	0.02%
5 Sound categorization	6.02
Middle Sound[b]	
4 Memory for words	0.27%
5 Sound categorization	2.29
End Sound[c]	
4 Memory for words	0.00%
5 Sound categorization	1.36

[a]Significance of contribution of sound categorization: $F = 24.24$, df 1,258, $p < .001$

[b]Significance of contribution of sound categorization: $F = 8.72$, df 1,258, $p < .005$

[c]Significance of contribution of sound categorization: $F = 5.12$, df 1,258, $p < .05$

Table 27 tells a similar story about this group's spelling levels. Once again the First Sound condition accounts for very much more of the variance than the other two conditions. All are significantly related to the children's spelling levels, but the relationship is much stronger and more significant in the case of alliteration.

We are now in a position to put the Primary Group's results together. Two major points need to be made. One is that it is only their skill with alliteration which is related to mathematical progress. The second—a related point—is that although all three sound conditions are related to reading and spelling (with the single exception of the End Sound condition and Schonell reading levels) the relationship is by far the strongest in the case of the alliteration, or First Sound, condition.

The focal point of any attempt to explain this very distinctive pattern must lie with the peculiar role of the alliteration

TABLE 26.   Multiple Regressions of the Three Sound Conditions for the Primary Group; Dependent Variable, Schonell Reading Age

Step	Additional Variance
All Regressions	
1 Chronological age	1.37%
2 E.P.V.T.	16.98
3 W.I.S.C.	7.89
First Sound[a]	
4 Memory for words	0.22%
5 Sound categorization	4.09
Middle Sound[b]	
4 Memory for words	0.27%
5 Sound categorization	3.00
End Sound[c]	
4 Memory for words	0.01%
5 Sound categorization	1.05

[a]Significance of contribution of sound categorization: $F = 15.08$, df 1,258, $p < .001$

[b]Significance of contribution of sound categorization: $F = 10.89$, df 1,258, $p < .005$

[c]Significance of contribution of sound categorization: $F = 3.71$, df 1,258, p = not significant

condition. This predicts all four educational tests remarkably well. Why does it do this with the Primary but not at all with the Nursery Group?

We have an explanation that seems convincing to us. One must remember that at the time of the initial tests the Primary Group had just arrived at their school (whereas, of course, the Nursery Group had not got there yet). We noticed that one of the most common features of the children's experiences in their early days at primary school was training in the first sound and the first letter of individual words. Most first-year classes would have, for example, "C" days when all the children had to remember to bring in objects with names beginning with the letter *c*. The letters changed weekly, with the result that these primary children were being given constant experience of grouping words by their first sound. They were being taught about it while the Nursery Group was not. It may

TABLE 27.   Multiple Regressions of the Three Sound Conditions for the Primary Group; Dependent Variable, Schonell Spelling Age

Step	Additional Variance
All Regressions	
1 Chronological age	1.77%
2 E.P.V.T.	11.33
3 W.I.S.C.	6.42
First Sound[a]	
4 Memory for words	0.20%
5 Sound categorization	7.90
Middle Sound[b]	
4 Memory for words	0.28%
5 Sound categorization	2.70
End Sound[c]	
4 Memory for words	0.01%
5 Sound categorization	1.40

[a]Significance of contribution of sound categorization: $F = 27.94$, df 1,258, $p < .001$

[b]Significance of contribution of sound categorization: $F = 8.93$, df 1,258, $p < .005$

[c]Significance of contribution of sound categorization: $F = 4.56$, df 1,258, $p < .05$

be no coincidence that, as we have already noted in chapter 4, alliteration seems to improve rapidly soon after children go to school (Bradley 1982).

Our idea is simply that, for this reason, our First Sound condition picked up more than just the Primary Group's natural ability to categorize sounds. It also measured their ability to learn at school. In the First Sound condition we were measuring how well they had learned something they were being taught. This is a plausible reason for this test's evident ability to predict educational progress along a wide front—mathematics as well as reading and spelling. If it is measuring how well a child learns from teaching it should predict how well he will do at every sort of lesson.

This seems to us the most likely reason why the Primary Group's alliteration scores were related to their progress in mathematics and why, also, they accounted for so much more of the variance in all four education tests than did the alliteration scores of the Nursery Group. The Primary Group was being taught about alliteration: the Nursery Group was not.

The analysis of the three conditions has done a great deal to show exactly what the connections are between children's ability to categorize words by their sounds and their later progress at school. As far as the Middle and End Sound conditions are concerned this connection is specific to reading and spelling, as our hypothesis predicted. The same is true of the First Sound condition as far as the Nursery Group is concerned. But in the Primary Group the alliteration condition obviously measured factors which were of great interest, but which were outside the range of our hypothesis.

We are content to have demostrated a specific connection between sound categorization and reading and spelling three years later in two sound conditions in the Primary Group and in all three sound conditions in the Nursery Group. A genuine relationship does exist, independently of intelligence, between children's ability to organize words into sound segments and the way in which they cope later on with learning about written language. In the next two chapters we shall establish that this relationship is a causal one.

Summary

With one exception all three sound categorization conditions account for a significant amount of the variance in both reading tests and in the spelling test as well. They do so independently of age, E.P.V.T., I.Q., and memory. The one exception was the relationship between the Primary Group's scores in the End Sound condition and Schonell reading, but since these scores were significantly related to Neale reading we can be reasonably sure that there is a connection between this condition and reading among these children. We conclude that a child's skill at isolating and categorizing sounds at the beginning, in the middle, and at the end of the word is strongly related to the way in which he learns to read and write.

In the Primary Group the alliteration condition accounts for much more of the variance in the children's eventual reading and spelling levels. In the Nursery Group that condition accounts for the smallest amount of variance: among these children it is the End Sound condition that accounts for most of the variance in reading and spelling.

There is also a difference in the two groups over the mathematics scores. The individual sound categorization conditions do not account for a significant amount of the variance in these scores in the Nursery Group. For them the connections between sound categorization and educational achievement remain specific to reading and spelling. In the Primary Group, on the other hand, there is a particularly strong relationship between the alliteration condition and mathematical skills. This condition, therefore, is strongly related to all four educational tests. The other two sound categorization conditions, however, are not significantly related to mathematical achievement.

Putting these results together we can see that all three forms of sound categorization are linked to progress in reading and spelling. In the case of the Nursery Group that relationship is always specific to reading and spelling. But in the Primary Group only the Middle and End Sound conditions are specifically connected to reading and spelling in that way. In this group the alliteration condition accounts for a highly significant amount of the variance on all four tests, including the mathematical one: we conclude that this condition given to primary school children in their first year at school acts as a measure of their ability to learn what they are taught, and thus predicts educational progress in a very general way.

CHAPTER 6

Training Study Methods

The Design

When we designed the training part of our project, we had two quite separate points in mind. The first has been mentioned already. In training studies it is absolutely essential (though all too rare) to have a control group that is treated in exactly the same way as the experimental group, apart from the experience which the experimenters think to be the crucial one.

To test the effects of training in sound categorization, our intention was to teach the children in the experimental group to group together pictures whose names had sounds in common. We had to find the correct control for this kind of categorization, and our solution was to give the children in one control group exactly the same amount of experience putting the same pictures into categories, but this time into conceptual categories. Some children categorized the pictures by sound, others by concept. Otherwise they were treated in exactly the same way.

Our second concern was with teaching methods. We had, of course, to have an experimental group whose children were trained to categorize sound and nothing else. That, together with the correct control, was an essential test of our hypothesis. But we were acutely aware that, if our aim was actually to teach children to read and not simply to test a hypothesis, we should not stop at training them in sound categorization alone. We felt that we should add another experimental group that reflected what we thought to be the best way of teaching a child to take advantage of sound categories when learning to read and write. For that we turned to tactual methods.

One of us (Bradley) has considerable experience of teaching backward readers. She has found that an extremely effective way of showing a child how to translate sound categories into reading and spelling is to use sets of plastic letters. The rationale is simple. Backward readers are often not at all successful in the aural medium, which to them seems particularly abstract and transitory. It is Bradley's experience that they are helped if, as they are being taught about sound categories, they are given something concrete and tangible to work with. The teacher uses the plastic letters to form one word, then another, and so on. All the words in the series have a sound, or more than one sound, in common, and the common sound or sounds are represented by a particular letter or letters. As the teacher finishes with one word either she or the child breaks it up, but always leaves the letter representing the sound it has in common with the next word untouched: new letters are added to it to form the next word, and then the whole process is repeated again several times. The effect is to make the relationship between the sounds that the words have in common and the letters that represent them very obvious. Alliteration and rhyme become, literally, tangible.

Since this seemed to us the best way to show the child how to use his knowledge of sound categories, we decided to add a group that was to be trained about sound categorization and was also to be helped with plastic letters. We decided to have two experimental groups and one control group. In one experimental group the children would have to be trained only about sound categories, and in the other they would, in addition, be taught how to encapsulate these categories with plastic letters. The control group would be trained in conceptual categories.

In the end we decided to add a fourth group—another control group of children who would be given no training at all. We wanted to see whether training in any categorization led to improvement on reading and spelling, and so we added a group that had no training.

So far we have talked about what experiences the different

groups were given, the independent variable. We should mention our dependent variables—the outcome measures—as well. These were the scores on the standardized tests of reading, spelling, and mathematics given at the end of the project, that were described in chapter 3. We thought it important to use the measure of mathematical skills as well, because our hypothesis was that training in sound categorization should improve reading and spelling but should have no appreciable effect on the children's success in mathematics.

The Training Procedures

Children in the Training Study

There are two points to make about the selection of children for this part of the project. The first is the way in which we decided who should be in the training study. This is very simple. We concentrated on children who were at the lower end of our sound categorization scores. Table 28 shows that the mean score for the children in the training study was well below the mean for the whole sample (see table 7).

The second point concerns the matching of the children in the different groups. It is extremely important in a study like ours that the children in the experimental and control groups should be matched as closely as possible on all relevant measures. The measures on which we did match the children in the groups were

1. sound categorization scores
2. E.P.V.T. scores
3. sex
4. whether or not they were in nursery school or primary school at the beginning of the project.

We included sixty-five children, and divided them into four groups.

Group I: Experimental (trained on sound categorization only), N = 13

Group II: Experimental (trained on sound categorization, and given experience with plastic letters), N = 13

Group III: Control (trained on conceptual categorization), N = 26

Group IV: Control (no training), N = 13

Our basic technique was to match individual children across groups. Although we had four groups we looked for sets of five children who were as close as possible on all four relevant measures. We dealt in sets of five rather than of four children

TABLE 28.   Details of the Four Groups in the Training Study

	Group				Significance of Difference F (df 3,61)[a]
	I	II	III	IV	
Number					
Nursery Group	3	3	6	3	
Primary Group	10	10	20	10	
Boys	8	8	16	8	
Girls	5	5	10	5	
Mean E.P.V.T.	103.0	103.0	102.3	102.7	1.0 NS
Sound Categorization Scores					
Nursery Group					
Total scores	13.0	12.7	12.7	14.3	1.17 NS
First Sound	4.0	4.3	2.8	5.0	2.43 NS
Middle Sound	4.0	4.3	5.7	5.0	2.54 NS
End Sound	4.3	4.7	4.2	5.0	0.18 NS
Primary Group					
Total scores	11.0	11.3	10.8	11.8	0.47 NS
First Sound	3.1	3.5	3.6	3.2	0.46 NS
Middle Sound	4.2	4.0	3.4	4.2	1.23 NS
End Sound	3.7	3.8	3.8	4.4	0.49 NS

[a]NS signifies a nonsignificant difference

because we decided to pair each child in the experimental group with a particular child in Group III (the crucial control group that was trained on conceptual categorization). This was why that group had twice as many children as the other groups. We carried out a series of one-way analyses of variance on each of the scores to compare the four groups, and, as table 28 shows, in no case was there any significant difference among the groups.

Procedure Common to All Trained Groups

The Sessions

The training spanned a two-year period. It began in the second year of the project when fourteen of the sixty-five children were still under six years old. The mean age of the group was seventy-three months (six years, one month), the youngest child being sixty-five months (five years, five months) and the oldest eighty-eight months (seven years, four months). Each child received forty training sessions. These were individual sessions: the children were always seen on their own.

The children in the two experimental and the one control group that received training (Groups I–III) were by this time scattered through sixteen different schools. A rota was set up for each of the fifty-two children being trained to be seen for one session a week in each week in which training took place. In the first year all the training was done by one person, but in the second year the rota was shared by two people, each of whom saw each child on alternate weeks. The child's place in the rota depended only on the location of his school and not at all on the group he happened to be in. It was a very tight schedule, tight enough to rule out the possibility of any child or group of children being seen more often than others. That kind of bias was simply not possible.

The control group (III) was seen for the same amount of time and was given exactly the same pictures and thus dealt with the same words as the group trained in sound categories alone (I). The only difference between the two was that one was trained to categorize by sound, the other by concept. Group II (trained in sound categories with the help of plastic letters) also received the same amount of attention, and dealt with the same pictures and words as these two groups.

Rationale for the Training

The training that these three groups were given in categorization was based on the methods developed by Bradley at the Park Hospital, Oxford, in her work with children with learning difficulties (Bradley 1980). Two principles lie at the heart of these methods. All the children in these three groups were given considerable experience with the first principle before they went on to the second.

The Principles
The first principle taught was that the same word can be categorized in the same way in different sets of words. To take an example from sound categories, *hen* starts with the same sound as *hat* and *hand,* and it also starts with the same sound as *hill* and *hair.* We taught the child exactly this, by giving him first a "hen-hat-hand" set and then a "hen-hill-hair" set. Examples of the sets of words used in sound category training with Groups I and II can be found in table 29.

The same thing applied to the first conceptual categories given to Group III. *Hen* was first categorized with *bat* and *man,* for example, and then immediately with *dog* and *leg.* Both sets belong to the category of "Living Things."

The second principle was that the same word can be categorized in different ways in successive sets of words. *Hen* starts with the same sound as *hat* and *hand,* ends with the same sound as *men* and *sun,* and has the same middle sound as *bed* and *leg.* In later stages of the training we demonstrated just this sort of thing with "hen-hat-hand" followed by "hen-men-sun" and "hen-bed-leg" sets.

This principle applied to conceptual categories too. *Hen,* for

TABLE 29. Examples of Sets of Words Used in the Sound Categories

First Sounds

b	c	h	n
bag	cat	hat	net
band	car	hand	nut
bat	cot	hen	nest
bed	cup	hair	nail
box	coat	hill	
ball	cake	hook	
book	cook		
bus			

Middle Sounds

a	e	i	o	u
bag	bed	pig	box	bus
cat	hen	fish	cot	cup
man	leg	hill	doll	gun
tap	net	pin	sock	nut
mat	peg		fox	sun
rat	ten		dog	

End Sounds

t	n	g
hat	man	bag
nut	hen	leg
net	gun	dog
coat	pin	pig
rat	sun	peg
cot	ten	

Rhyming Groups

bat	hen	band
mat	men	hand
cat	pen	land
rat	ten	sand
hat		

example, was categorized with *man* and *leg* ("Living Things"), with *fox* and *dog* ("Animals"), and then with *pig* and *duck* ("Farm Animals").

Broad versus Narrow Categories

Another decision we made was to start with categories that contained many obvious instances. This was necessary because the first principle (categorizing the same word in the same way with many different sets of words) demands many instances. Otherwise one runs out of sets of words.

As far as sound categories are concerned, it is easier to find many examples of words that start with the same sound than to find words that rhyme. For this reason the two groups trained in sound categorization started with alliteration and then went on to rhyme when they were taught the first principle. In their case there was another reason for this order; we find that it is actually easier to explain to young children what one wants with sets of words which start with the same sound than it is with rhyming sets.

Table 30 contains examples of the conceptual categories used with Group III, the control group receiving training in categorizing words by concept rather than by sound. The first broad categories for the control group were "Things Inside," "Things Outside," "Living Things," and "Things Made." These were later divided up into narrower subcategories. For example, one of the first categories, "Living Things," includes other categories like "People," "Animals," "Farm Animals," and "Animals That Swim."

Thus the progression from broad to narrower categories while the first principle was being taught prepared the child for the second principle, in which he would have to deal with relatively broad and relatively narrow categories in close succession; with alliteration, for example, and then with rhyme, or with "Things Outside" and then with "Farm Animals."

The training for all the groups proceeded in similar fashion in the individual sessions over the two years. A more detailed

Broad Categories

Things Inside	Things Outside	Living Things	Things Made	Transport
mat	band	bat	bag	bus
bag	hill	cat	box	car
bed	net	hand	ball	van
box	nest	leg	coat	leg
book	land	hen	hat	foot
cot	sand	hair	nail	train
hook	nut	rat	pen	boat
cup	sun	men		ship
jam	gun	dog		
cake	rock	pig		
cook	tree	man		
tap				

Narrower Categories

Living Things

Things Inside		Animals				People	Parts of People
Kitchen	Bedroom	Pets	Farm	Wild	That Swim	People	Parts of People
cup	bed	dog	hen	bat	duck	man	hand
mug	cot	cat	pig	fox	fish	boy	leg
jam	mat	fish	duck	frog	frog	girl	hair
cake	book		goat	toad	toad	cook	feet
peg	pin		sheep			band	teeth
cook	hook					men	
						queen	

Things Made

Clothes	Transport with Wheels
hat	bus
coat	car
boot	van
sock	train

exposition of some points of the procedure follows. It will concentrate on the sound categorization training.

Procedure Common to Both Experimental Groups (I and II)

The two experimental groups received exactly the same treatment for the first twenty sessions. In the earliest sessions, the children were taught to categorize words on the basis of common sounds using pictures of familiar objects. Some examples of the pictures used are given in figures 1 and 2. No written work at all was done during the training study.

The different categories of sound were introduced in the same order for everyone, but each child progressed at his own rate. For the reasons already given the First Sound categories were introduced first as these were the ones with the largest sets of words, and this made it easier to vary sets and demonstrate the first principle. For this reason the first category introduced was words beginning with *b*.

Some of the picture cards from this group were spread out on the table. The child was asked to say the names of the objects in the pictures: "bat, bus, bed, book, ball." Then he was asked to say the words again, and to listen to them. Then he was asked to say them yet again, listening to see if he could hear anything the same about them. He was encouraged to discover that they all started with the same sound, and that the sound was *b*. This concept was reinforced by repeating the task in various ways, and the first way was of course to repeat it using different picture cards.

The next was to introduce one or more pictures of objects whose names started with a different sound, such as a cat. The child was then given the following tasks:

1. "Find me pictures of things which start the same as this one (show picture of bus)."
2. "Find me pictures of things that start with *b*."

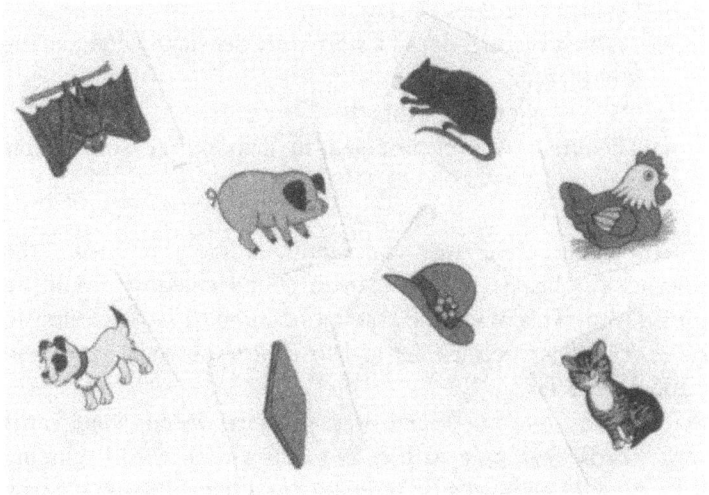

Fig. 1. Groups I and II categorize "bat," "rat," "cat," "hat," and "mat" as rhyming words; Group III categorizes "bat," "pig," "rat," "hen," "cat," and "dog" as animals.

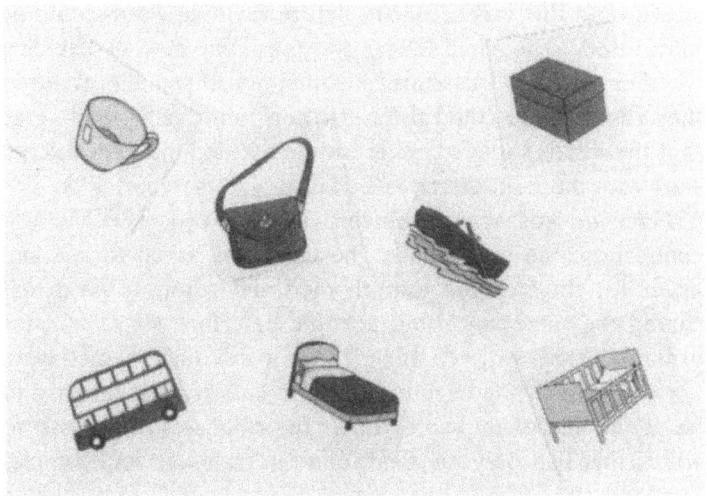

Fig. 2. Groups I and II categorize "bag," "bed," "boat," "bus," and "box" as words that start with the *b* sound; Group III categorizes "bag," "bed," "cot," "box," and "cup" as objects typically found indoors.

3. "Which one doesn't start with *b*?"
4. "Which picture doesn't start with the same sound as the others?"
5. "Which pictures go together?"
6. The child was encouraged to give the reason for his choice.

When the child was consistently correct in giving the reasons for his decision, the next sound category would be introduced. This made the task more complex (*b* was followed by *c, h,* and *n*) because he had to choose between more and more categories.

The "odd one out" game was also introduced: some cards with words beginning with *b* and one with a word beginning with *c* would be placed on the table, and the child asked to say which card did not belong with the others, and to give a reason for his choice.

At this stage teaching about the second principle began. The children had become accustomed to terms like *word* and *sound,* and this was necessary before rhyming words could be introduced. The child was now given the task of deciding whether sets of words shared a common first sound or whether they rhymed. He could listen to "hen" and "pen," and agree that the words sounded alike. But he decided that they did not start with the same sound.

Once he was able to do this, he had to deal with a new connection, the end sound. The child was asked to say, and listen to, three words that rhymed and a fourth word that shared the same vowel but not the same final consonant, for example, "hat, cat, rat, man." The words that rhymed were not the same at the beginning, so the sound connection had to be at the end of the word. Later the child was introduced to words that had only the final sound in common: for example, *man* and *pin.*

Finally the child was introduced to sets of words that

shared the same middle vowel sound. He was asked to say, and listen to, three words that rhymed and a fourth word that shared the same final consonant but not the same vowel, for example, "hat, mat, rat, cot." As the words could not be categorized on the basis of first sounds, and all had the same end sound, the word that sounded different had to be different somewhere else. Children who became adept at categorizing words in this way were eventually introduced to sets of words like *man* and *cat,* which shared only the same middle vowel sound.

As each child became more skilled, examples were given aurally without the help of pictures. He was now asked to:

1. Produce words sharing a common sound.
2. Say which sound was shared by a group of words.
3. Choose the odd one out of four spoken words given the sound in common.
4. Choose the odd one out of four spoken words not given the sound in common.
5. Identify the sound common to three out of four spoken words.

Because each child went at his own speed many never got as far as this on the program. This was especially true of the children who were slow learners, or who seemed to have particular problems attending to the sounds in spoken words. But our plan was that they should all be given the tasks in the same order. The one exception to our rule was a girl with a speech problem who made poor progress on the First Sound categories. It seemed possible that this was because of her inability to pronounce the beginning of many words. She was given a fresh start with rhyming categories, which she found much easier, and then returned later and more successfully to categorizing words on the basis of common first sounds.

Procedure with Experimental Group II

The children in both experimental groups followed this same program. But in the second half of the training sessions Group II were taught with the help of plastic alphabet letters as well.

Whenever a new sound category was introduced, it was demonstrated first with the help of the picture cards in the normal way. But the child then made each word in the set with plastic letters. (All of the children had by this time attended school for at least two years, and they were quite familiar with the alphabet.)

The letters were in a box on the table and the child had to select the letters he needed to make the first word. He was then asked to make the next word in the set.

To begin with the children tended to put away the letters that they had used for the first word at this point and to start the second word from scratch. But they soon learned that the second word needed many of the same letters as the first word. On the whole it was not long before they discovered, when one word was *hat* and the next *cat* for example, that they need only alter one letter to change one word into the other. The unit that was common to the spoken words stayed on the table while the other letters changed.

The sessions were still the same length as before, but naturally less time was spent using the picture cards.

Procedure with Control Group III

The training program for the control group was based on the same two principles, using the same words and the same picture cards. Again the children learned to group the words together, but this time the words were grouped into conceptual categories. The program and the training tasks were similar to those given to Groups I and II, except that the children had to search for conceptual connections among the sets of words.

Summary

Sixty-five children were involved in a training study that lasted for two years—the middle two years of our four-year project. They were divided into four groups, one receiving training in sound categorization only, one in sound categorization and in constructing words with alphabetic letters, and one in conceptual categorization, while one was not trained at all.

All the children trained were taught first to categorize particular words repeatedly in the same way in different sets of words, and then later to categorize the same word in many different ways.

CHAPTER 7

Training Study Results

We have established that there is a definite and strong relationship between sound categorization and reading and writing skills. But we cannot be sure that the relationship is a causal one, and as far as we can see that kind of certainty can only come through a training study.

We have already described the design and procedures of our quite considerable training experiment that lasted for a period of two years and employed careful controls. We can now turn to its results. Our outcome measures, or dependent variables, were the four groups' final scores in the standardized reading, spelling, and mathematical tests. Thus we were monitoring whether our training procedures actually improved the child's achievement in the classroom. We wanted to see whether we were affecting variables in real life and not just in the laboratory.

Table 31 summarizes the effects of the training. The reading and spelling scores show very similar patterns. The two experimental groups consistently fared a great deal better than both of the control groups. This suggests that training in sound categorization does have a positive effect on learning to read and write. Furthermore, the differences between experimental and control groups looked much smaller in the case of the mathematics test. We seem to have found that training in sound categorization does improve reading and spelling quite markedly, and that it has a much smaller effect on math.

Let us look at the groups in more detail. First there is the question of how training in sound categorization only (Group I) compares to training in conceptual categorization only (Group

III). Table 31 shows that Group I was consistently ahead of Group III, and also that this difference was greater for reading and spelling than it was for math. This consistent superiority of Group I over Group III in reading and spelling does at last establish a causal connection between sound categorization and written language.

We can also see that there is a pronounced and consistent difference between the two experimental groups. The children in Group II, who were taught in sound categorization but who were also taught with plastic letters in the second half of the training program, ended up reading and spelling far in advance of the children in Group I, whose training was confined to categorizing sounds. It seems that training in sound categories is particularly effective when the connection between these categories and the alphabet is made very explicit. This is a conclusion of some practical importance.

Two further things need be said about this difference between the two experimental groups. One is that it was at its greatest in the spelling scores. The children trained in sound categories with the help of plastic letters really did extraordinarily well. Their spelling scores were well above average for

TABLE 31.   Mean Scores of Groups Participating in the Training Study

	Groups			
	I	II	III	IV
I.Q.	97.15	101.23	102.34	100.15
Schonell reading age (months)	92.23	96.96	88.48	85.70
Neale reading age (months)	93.47	99.77	89.09	85.70
Schonell spelling age (months)	85.97	98.81	81.76	75.15
Mathematics (ratio score)	91.27	91.09	87.99	84.13

Note: the reading and spelling are adjusted for two covariants—age and I.Q.—and the mathematics for one—I.Q.

their age even though their I.Q.'s were close to the mean. Their spelling ages were thirteen months ahead of their nearest rivals, the children in Group I, trained in sound categories only. Even more impressively, they were ahead of the children in Group IV, who received no training, by twenty-three months. This is a particularly striking difference. We have indeed established a powerful educational technique.

The second point about the superiority of Group II over Group I is that it is specific to reading and spelling. There was no difference between the two groups in mathematical skills at all. The plastic letters help reading and particularly spelling, but do not touch other educational skills.

One further consistent result needs to be mentioned. The untrained control group was worse than all three groups on all four educational measures. There are two possible ways of explaining this difference. One is that it is something to do with the attention that Groups I, II, and III received. The other is more interesting: it is that those three groups, but not Group IV, were all trained in some form of categorization and that this helped them intellectually, whether the categories in question were of sounds or of concepts. We favor the second of these two hypotheses, but we cannot definitely say that it is right.

So far we have simply described the mean results. We turn now to their analysis. If you want to find out whether groups in a training study really are different from each other the natural technique is the one-way analysis of variance. But sometimes it is not possible to match your groups from the start on all possible relevant variables. In this case it is far better to use a one-way analysis of covariance; this works out what the groups' scores would have been had they all been equal on these other variables.

We had matched our five groups very carefully on all the variables that we had measured at the time the training started, and we have described this matching in chapter 7. However, there were two variables that might influence the children's educational scores and that we could not control at the outset of the training study. These were (1) the child's I.Q., because this was not measured until the end of the project (note that we did match the groups very closely on their initial E.P.V.T. scores); and (2) the child's actual chronological age at the time of the final tests: we could not ensure that this was the same for all children because the final testing stretched over many months and our schedule was constrained by the schools' own arrangements.

We decided to do four analyses of covariance. Each analysis measured differences in one of the four educational tests, and in each analysis the scores were adjusted for two covariants: I.Q. and age at time of testing. We could therefore assume that all four groups were in effect equal in terms of their initial scores in the sound categorization tests, their initial E.P.V.T. quotients, their sex, whether they were from the Nursery or Primary Group, their I.Q., and their age on the final tests.

The results of these analyses can be described very simply. There were significant differences among the groups in the two reading tests and in the spelling test but not in the mathematics test. The group differences were significant in the case of reading (Schonell: $F = 5.23$; df 3,58; $p < .003$. Neale: $F = 7.80$; df 3,58; $p < .001$) and of spelling ($F = 12.18$; df 3,58; $p < .001$) but not in the case of mathematics ($F = 1.64$; df 3,39; $p = NS$).

Posttests (Tukey's H.S.D.) showed that Group II was significantly better than both control groups (Groups III and IV) in Schonell and in Neale reading ($p < .05$) and in Schonell spelling ($p < .01$). There was no significant difference between Groups I and II (the two groups trained in sound categorization) in the two reading tests, but Group II did surpass Group I in spelling ($p < .05$).

Although Group I's reading and spelling scores were always ahead of Group III's this difference did not reach significance in the posttests. But the consistent three-to-four-month superiority of Group I over Group III does strongly suggest that training in sound categorization affects progress in reading and spelling. Group I was significantly better than Group IV (the untrained control group) in the two reading tests and in the spelling test ($p < .05$). On the other hand there were no significant differences at all between the two control groups (III and IV).

The effects of training in sound categorization therefore are specific to reading and spelling, and they are significant. So the results of the training study provide very strong evidence for our causal hypothesis. Training in sound categorization improves reading and spelling. The effect is a specific one.

Summary

The group trained to categorize sounds only (I) read and spelled better than the group trained only with conceptual categories (III).

The reading and spelling levels of both these groups were surpassed by those of the group trained both in sound categories and in the use of plastic letters (II).

These training effects were fairly specific to reading and spelling. No significant training effects were found in the mathematics scores.

CHAPTER 8

Individual Differences

One of the reasons for looking at measures of young children's sound categorization skills was to see whether these measures might help with the prediction of success and failure in learning to read. We knew that children who were already demonstrably behind in learning to read and spell were on the whole very bad at detecting rhyme and alliteration (Bradley and Bryant 1978). But we did not know whether this was true, relatively speaking, before they began to read, and so we had no idea whether our tests of sound categorization could be used to help predict who would do well and who badly at reading if the measures were given to preschool children.

We must note at the outset that on their own our tests will never be anything like perfect predictors. There were, as we noted in chapters 4 and 5, consistent and significant relationships between sound categorization and reading and spelling. But learning to read and write is a complicated business to which many factors contribute. Although our sound categorization tests did account for a significant proportion of the variance in the scores in the reading and spelling tests, the figure was never more than 10 percent and sometimes as little as 4 percent of that variance (after intelligence and verbal level had been controlled). There are many important influences other than the particular one we have been pursuing.

This means that on its own a sound categorization score can never hope to be a good predictor of children who will do unusually well or unusually badly at reading and spelling. When we look, as we shall do in this chapter, at the sound categorization tests as predictors on their own we must be prepared for fairly slim results.

Nevertheless there is an important question here. So far we have given it only a partial answer. We know that, overall, rhyming skills are related to future success in learning to read. That was established by the multiple regressions described in chapters 4 and 5. However, these demonstrated a general relationship, which is obviously extremely important but which tells us little about the few extreme cases—little, that is, about the interesting handful of children in our sample who were exceptionally good or exceptionally weak at categorizing sounds in our initial tests.

We want, of course, to know whether unusual scores in sound categorization will predict success or failure in learning to read. But, put as simply as this, the question is altogether too crude. Obviously there are children who will do remarkably well (or remarkably badly) on any test, sound categorization included, and will learn particularly well (or particularly poorly) when it is time for them to learn to read. These children's success and failure would be predicted at least as well by other measures, such as the W.I.S.C. and the E.P.V.T.; if this were all, measures of sound categorization would add not a jot to our ability to predict success or failure.

We are now in a position to put our question about prediction in its final form. We want to find out whether sound categorization adds any additional predictive power *on top of other established measures*. Let us phrase this question in terms of the two main established measures we used in addition to our tests of sound categorization at the beginning, and of reading and spelling skills, at the end of the project. These were E.P.V.T., which we administered at the same time as the original tests of sound categorization when the children were four and five years old, and W.I.S.C., which coincided with the final assessments of reading and spelling skills. Our rephrased question is whether any child whose sound categorization scores are unusually good (or unusually poor) after both his E.P.V.T. score and his age at the time of the test are taken into account will learn to read and to spell unusually well (or unusually unsuccessfully) after his I.Q. has been taken into account.

This new question poses two problems. One is how to take the other variables into account. The other is what one means by "unusually good" or "bad" in sound categorization and in reading and spelling. Fortunately the solutions to both problems are quite simple.

When we calculated whether a child did better or worse in the sound categorization tests than would normally be expected, we first worked out (using the regression between sound categorization and both E.P.V.T. and age) what his sound categorization score should have been given his age and his E.P.V.T. score. Then we looked to see what his actual sound categorization score was, and if it was far above or below the expected score we regarded the child as unusual.

We used the regression between reading or spelling and W.I.S.C. and age in just the same way when we considered whether children were particularly good (or particularly poor) readers and spellers. We decided that they were unusual if their reading or spelling scores diverged quite a bit from the level predicted from regressions on their age and I.Q.

This brings us to the second problem, which was how far from the expected score the child had to be in order to qualify as unusual. Any decision about this kind of distinction has to be arbitrary. There is no generally accepted fiat for saying when a child must be regarded as exceptional. Indeed there are good reasons for avoiding a rigid criterion. For our purposes we simply chose one standard deviation as the dividing point. In other words if the child scored one standard deviation or more above or below his expected sound categorization or his reading and spelling score we treated him as exceptionally good or bad at this particular skill. Similarly if his reading or spelling scores were one standard deviation away from the level that would have been expected from his age and I.Q. we treated him as a good or a poor reader/speller.

Having made these decisions the business of looking at the capacity of our sound categorization tests as predictors of success and failure in reading was straightforward. We simply looked to see whether exceptionally good sound categorizers would end up as exceptionally skilled readers/spellers, and exceptionally poor sound categorizers the other way. We set about finding whether children whose sound categorization scores were one standard deviation away from their expected score would also reach a reading level that was one standard deviation or more higher than their I.Q. would predict. Of course we asked the same question about the children whose sound categorization scores fell one standard deviation or more below the expected level: we wanted to know whether they would become poor readers, and from the point of view of the starting point of the study this was the more important question. We wanted to know whether we could predict which children would have learning difficulties, children whose reading and spelling were poor despite normal intelligence.

We decided to take one more precaution. We already knew that some of the children in our training groups, all of whom had been at the low end of our original sound categorization scores, had done rather well at reading and spelling. Furthermore our controls had shown that this was something to do with the training which these children had received. It seemed to us that these particular children's scores might throw our results out. After all, our question was about predicting whether or not children who were receiving *no out of the ordinary teaching* would become unexpectedly good or poor readers. So we decided to eliminate all the children who had actually been trained—the 52 children in Groups I, II, and III—from our analysis, and to turn our attention to the remaining 316 children in our sample.

Before considering the results it is worth reminding ourselves that for the rest of this chapter we shall be concentrating on a relatively small group of children. We shall turn most of our attention to the extreme cases. Our question is whether children whose sound categorization scores were one or more standard deviation above or below the level which would have been expected from their age and E.P.V.T. scores turn out to be either successes or failures as readers and spellers. But there are not all that many such children. On that criterion, 53 of the 316 children were particularly good in the sound categorization tests and only 25 particularly bad. (The asymmetry is due to the fact that a high proportion of the 52 children in the training groups, whom we are not considering here, had low sound categorization scores.)

Table 32 shows how many of these few exceptional children went on to become good or poor readers. As we expected these results are rather slender. Rather few (16 out of 53, or 30 percent) of the children who were at the start unexpectedly good at sound categorizing became exceptionally good readers. A slightly smaller proportion of those who initially produced poor sound categorization scores became exceptionally poor readers (7 out of 25, or 28 percent). This last result is slightly disappointing, given that one of the main reasons for the project was our earlier study (Bradley and Bryant 1978) that demonstrated a pronounced weakness in sound categorization among children with learning difficulties. We need to remember that the children with the lowest initial scores on sound categorization have been excluded from this analysis. Nevertheless we have to face the fact that our sound categorization test on its own might not be a particularly effective way of predicting eventual learning difficulties.

TABLE 32.   Predictive Value of Sound Categorization Scores for Neale Reading Scores

Expected Neale Reading Score	Expected Sound Categorization Scores		
	One S.D. Above ($N = 53$)	Within One S.D. ($N = 238$)	One S.D. Below ($N = 25$)
One S.D. or more above	16 (30%)	35 (15%)	1 (4%)
One S.D. or more below	3 (6%)	37 (16%)	7 (28%)

This is only one test. However, our other reading test goes much the same way. Table 33 shows much the same pattern with the Schonell reading test scores. Again a third or less of the children who produced unusual scores on the initial sound categorization tests became unusually good or unusually poor readers. All that remains are the spelling scores, which go very much the same way, as table 34 shows.

Our three tests of reading/spelling produce a very consistent story. If we look at the extreme scorers in our sound categorization tests and in the reading and spelling tests, we find that roughly a quarter to a third of those who produced unusual scores in the sound categorization test became exceptional readers or spellers. So, on its own our test will not be particularly useful as a way of predicting success or failure in reading

TABLE 33. Predictive Value of Sound Categorization Scores for Schonell Reading Scores

	Expected Sound Categorization Scores		
Expected Schonell Reading Score	One S.D. Above ($N = 53$)	Within One S.D. ($N = 238$)	One S.D. Below ($N = 25$)
One S.D. or more above	17 (32%)	31 (13%)	1 (4%)
One S.D. or more below	3 (6%)	40 (17%)	6 (24%)

TABLE 34. Predictive Value of Sound Categorization Scores for Schonell Spelling Scores

	Expected Sound Categorization Scores		
Expected Schonell Spelling Scores	One S.D. Above ($N = 53$)	Within One S.D. ($N = 238$)	One S.D. Below ($N = 25$)
One S.D. or more above	15 (28%)	37 (16%)	0
One S.D. or more below	2 (4%)	42 (18%)	7 (28%)

and spelling. Its scores will not tell us with any degree of certainty, for example, whether individual children will eventually experience learning difficulties. But it will spot some of these children and this is no more than we expected or indeed wanted.

We had after all set ourselves a very difficult task because we had controlled both for E.P.V.T. and for I.Q. We were in effect trying to make not the crude prediction of who would become poor readers, but the much more sophisticated prediction of who would read below the level predicted by their I.Q. We set ourselves against I.Q. and tried to predict reading skills despite it. Nobody as far as we know has managed to do that at all successfully, and we, it must be said, have had a modicum of success.

The proportion of children who, on our measures, were weak sound categorizers and went on to become poor readers/spellers was far higher than the proportion of children whose sound categorization scores were within one standard deviation of their expected score. For example, table 32 shows that 28 percent of our weak sound categorizers went on to become weak readers on our Neale measure (i.e., one standard deviation or more below what would have been expected from their I.Q. score), whereas only 16 percent of those whose sound categorization scores were within one standard deviation of their expected level became backward readers. The equivalent figures for the Schonell reading test (table 33) were respectively 24 percent and 17 percent and for the Schonell spelling test (table 34) 28 percent and 18 percent.

Even at their weakest point as predictors our sound categorization measures do better than no measures at all. The fact that they are by no means perfect even at their strongest point strengthens our belief that reading and spelling are both complicated activities that make many different demands, and so can only be predicted with a variety of tests. We are reasonably sure that our measures will be a valuable addition to such a battery.

There is one other question to be asked about the prediction of individual cases. So far we have put the Nursery and Primary Groups together, although the predictions were of course made on the basis of regressions run for the two groups separately. In other words we have been asking what happened to children whose original sound categorization scores were remarkable *for their own group,* nursery or primary.

We have not yet considered whether one group's original sound categorization scores were better predictors of unusual reading levels than the other's. Table 35, which deals just with percentages, demonstrates that the scores which we garnered from the Nursery Group were better predictors, particularly when it came to predicting unusually good readers.

These results are rather complicated and need to be treated with some caution because the numbers involved are sometimes very small. For example, only seven children in the Nursery Group were poor readers on our criterion. Nevertheless table 35 does suggest some interesting things.

It looks as though the sound categorization tests which we

TABLE 35. Predictive Value of Sound Categorization Scores for Reading/Spelling Scores, by Percentage

| | Expected Sound Categorization Scores | | | |
| | Nursery Group | | Primary Group | |
	One S.D. Above ($N = 15$)	One S.D. Below ($N = 7$)	One S.D. Above ($N = 38$)	One S.D. Below ($N = 18$)
Neale Reading				
One s.d. above	46	0	23	5
One s.d. below	0	14	7	33
Schonell Reading				
One s.d. above	53	0	23	5
One s.d. below	0	14	7	33
Schonell Spelling				
One s.d. above	40	6	23	0
One s.d. below	0	28	2	27

gave to the four-year-old children (the Nursery Group) were really rather good at picking up those children who would eventually become good readers. The percentage success in this case ranged between 40 and 53 percent. On the other hand these same tests were very weak indeed at predicting reading failure. The successful rate of prediction of poor readers ranged from as low as 14 percent to 28 percent.

Turning to the sound categorization tests given to five-year-old children (the Primary Group) we can see that the prediction rate for good readers/spellers is not so high (23 percent) as the Nursery Group's. The tests given to the Primary Group were slightly better at predicting poor readers (27–33 percent).

It is gratifying that the Nursery Group's scores were so good at telling whether they would become unusually good readers. We consider this to be a valuable result. If it turns out to be reliable (one must remember that there were as few as fifteen unusually good readers in this group) we will have discovered a useful addition to ways of predicting educational success.

We cannot say the same about predicting reading failure. The tests given to the Nursery Group do not seem to select poor readers to any extent at all (though again there are reasons for caution because the numbers involved—only seven poor readers in this group—were very small indeed). The Primary Group's scores manage to pick out the poor readers/spellers with much more success. But even here we must be cautious. We could still only say that a child who at the age of five scores poorly on these tests has a 33 percent chance of becoming a poor reader. That is something, but not enough on its own. Other tests are needed too. Results like these support our belief that learning to read and spell is a complicated business which involves a number of different skills, of which we are tapping only one.

In general we can conclude that someone with unusual sound categorization scores is more likely to turn out to be an exceptional reader/speller than someone whose sound categorization scores are near normal. This can only mean that our

sound categorization scores do increase our ability to predict
success and failure in reading and spelling over and above
traditional measures. On their own they will not be particularly compelling, but combined with other measures that tap
the other processes involved in learning to read and to spell
they will have their uses.

Summary

We wanted to see whether unusual scores in the sound categorization tests could be used to predict who would do exceptionally well or exceptionally badly at reading and spelling. We
looked at the children whose sound categorization scores were
more than one standard deviation above or below the level
that would have been expected on the basis of their age and
their verbal levels, but did not include the fifty-two children
with low sound categorization scores who received training.

We found out how many of these went on to read better or
worse than would be expected from their age and intelligence.
We defined those children whose reading was more than one
standard deviation above or below the level that would be
expected from their age and I.Q. as good or poor readers.

Between a quarter and a third of those who scored unusually well or poorly in the sound categorization tests went on to
do particularly well or badly at reading and spelling.

The patterns of prediction turned out to be different for the
two groups. The sound categorization tests we gave to the
four-year-old children predicted reading and spelling successes
rather effectively. But they did not do at all well at predicting
reading and spelling failure. The tests given to the older children were somewhat better at predicting failure than success.

We concluded that our sound categorization tests can be
used to help predict success and failure, but only in conjunc-
tion with other tests.

CHAPTER 9

Individual Children

Our results have demonstrated three main things. The first is that children's early skills with rhyme have an effect on their progress in reading and spelling—an effect that is causal in nature. The second is that this sort of skill can be taught. The third is that the causal determinant that interests us is just one of the many influences that affect children's understanding of written language. Now we wish to describe examples of particular children whom we think illustrate each of these conclusions quite clearly.

David

We start with a boy whose sound categorization scores were low and who, as far as we could see, should on all other indications have been a successful reader. But he was not, and we attribute his reading failure to his insensitivity to rhyme and alliteration.

His sound categorization scores at initial testing (when he was five years, four months old) were only 3 correct trials out of 10 (First Sound), 3 (Middle Sound), and 7 (End Sound). These are low scores, especially when one considers his E.P.V.T. score of 112, which put him at the seventy-ninth percentile. At the time of the initial tests we noted his excellent language skills: his first sentence to us was "Did you notice that there was an old bell outside?", which is a sophisticated construction for a six year old. He came from a middle-class, caring family and was in an excellent school in a good residential area. He had a steady demeanor and a clear, bright approach. The school's checks at five and seven years did show some perceptuo-motor difficulty when he was five but this was gone by the time he was seven.

Because of his relatively low score he was included in the training study, but was put in the control group (III) that received training in conceptual categorization. For the first eighteen months of this training we found ourselves wondering why he had fared so badly in sound categorization, as he did well on the conceptual training.

During the second year of the training his teacher asked us if we had any comments to make about him. She was concerned about his lack of progress in school. His parents had also begun to worry, and had asked the family doctor to refer him to a clinical psychologist. David may have been affected by this concern, because in the eighteenth month of the training he began, unexpectedly, to have difficulty concentrating and did not categorize the words at all well. But this difficult phase lasted for only four weeks, and there was never any other indication that he had any problems at all.

At final testing he was eight years, six months old. On the standardized tests of reading he scored at the seven years, eleven months level (Neale accuracy) and eight years (Schonell), while his spelling had only reached six years, eleven months. On the W.I.S.C./R. his full-scale I.Q. score was 122, with no noticeable discrepancy between verbal and performance scores. This meant that in effect he had already fallen a year behind in reading and two years behind in spelling. As he was a very bright little boy it was easy to see why his teacher and parents were concerned about his progress. We could not find any explanation at all for his problems apart from his evident difficulty with sound categorization.

Tom

Our next example is very different. It concerns a boy whose initial scores in the sound categorization task were high. These scores would seem to predict that he would fare very well academically, but this was not the case. There do seem to be other good reasons for his failure, and his case serves to illustrate that there is more to reading than simply sound categorization.

Tom came from a one-parent family and was first tested at age four years, eleven months in the nursery class. He did not find the sound categorization task difficult, scoring 7, 7, and 9 in the First, Middle, and End Sound conditions respectively, which was slightly above the mean for the Nursery Group. He had no particular problem remembering the words, or with reciting a nursery rhyme when asked. His score on the E.P.V.T. put him at the sixty-first percentile for his age. Although his speech seemed rather immature there was no indication from his performance on these tests that he would have any problem with learning to read or to spell.

Tom moved into the school at the beginning of the following term a few months later. He should have been accustomed to the school since his nursery class had been there. However he failed half the items of a school screening check of communication skills and more than half the items in a similar check of emotional and social factors.

It emerged that he had a chaotic home life. He was referred by the school to the school psychological services, but the family moved and he with it to a different school that followed a less structured routine than his first school. He made no progress; the psychological service recommended a special school with the formal structured routine that was thought to be suitable for disturbed children.

His mother remarried and they moved again; he came back to his first school. A hearing test at the age of six years, one month showed a mild conductive loss in both ears. He was taken away from school again by his mother during term time to visit a relative. (His new father did not go.)

At the time of the final tests when he was eight years, eight months old, his scores on the standardized tests of reading and spelling were low: Neale reading, seven years, six months (accuracy); Schonell reading, seven years, two months; Schonell spelling, seven years. Yet his intelligence level was high (W.I.S.C. 136). Although his scores on the sound categorization test had been within the average range for the Nursery Group, his Schonell reading age was now thirty-eight months below that predicted for his age and intelligence.

At this time he failed to produce words that rhymed or began with the same sound as stimulus words. The production of rhyme is something that happens very early in the young child's language play. It is possible that this stage of language development could have been affected by his early hearing loss, or even by lack of stimulation and reinforcement in his unstable home environment.

We cannot in any way be certain about these things. But the school personnel were in no doubt that his chaotic home life had had a very serious effect upon his progress, and it is very possible that his hearing loss had affected this as well. On the basis of his reasonable performance in the sound categorization task, and his intellectual ability, we should not have predicted his lack of progress in reading and spelling. However, given the other circumstances, we do not find his failure at all surprising.

Ben

So far we have looked at two examples of reading failure, one of which could be described in terms of our hypothesis about sound categorization, the other of which could not. Those two cases neatly illustrate how the variable which interests us might be a crucial factor in some cases, and not in others.

We can also use individual cases as instances of another important part of our project, the effect of training in sound categorization. As it happens the two examples we shall quote were both epileptic boys. One was trained in sound categorization, the other was not.

Although there were differences in the boys' home backgrounds, and one was more intelligent than the other, they had a lot in common beside their epilepsy. Both boys were identified on our sound categorization test as having particular difficulty identifying sound similarities in spoken words. Both boys were under observation for their epilepsy, and on drugs for similar and concurrent periods of time during the study. They were also each a considerable source of concern at school, and of anxiety at home, and in both cases the help and advice of outside agencies had been sought. The boys are of particular interest to us because having identified them we assigned one to a sound categorization training group (Group II), and the other to a control training group (Group IV), and we did so before we knew about their epilepsy. As it turned out we had two children with similar difficulties, only one of whom received the training that we believe to be appropriate.

This was Ben. He was a noticeable character. When we were testing the children at his school he continually walked through the testing room banging the door loudly. He was a large boy who was not the least bit inhibited and who tended to be disruptive. He was ebullient in the test situation, but easily distracted.

At the initial tests, despite his confidence and age (five years, eleven months) he scored only 4 (First Sound), 3 (Middle Sound), and 6 (End Sound) in the sound categorization tasks. Yet his score on the E.P.V.T. (102) put him at the fifty-fifth percentile for his age group. He was selected for the training study and was assigned to Group II (sound categorization with plastic letters).

We soon found that we had our hands full with Ben in the training session, but were relieved to find that our problems were not unique. He was a master at manipulating the staff; he would tell his teacher that he "felt funny" and that his mother must be sent for. He would be referred to the head teacher, who sensibly used his discretion on each occasion. But Ben assured his parents that he was having "funny turns" in school, and played his parents off against the school staff. The school sought advice on handling him, and his parents did too. We found it absolutely essential to structure not only the training session, but the walk from his classroom to the training room. At other times he seemed completely lethargic, and was not only no trouble but seemed quite unwell. These contrasting features in his behavior seemed related to the changes in his drug program.

Ben responded to the structured training program; he particularly liked to be successful and would "switch off" if he was not, or if he was bored, or if he didn't feel cooperative. He would manipulate the session if he could. At final testing he was eight years, ten months old. His reading score on the Neale was eight years, seven months (comprehension), and on the Schonell eight years, four months. His Schonell spelling age was eight years, seven months.

His overall I.Q. was average. His scores on the W.I.S.C./R. were Verbal 88, Performance 109, Full-Scale I.Q. 98. So his performance on all the standardized tests was within four months of scores predicted on the basis of his age and intelligence. In view of his behavior, the school difficulties in handling, and his periods on drug trials and in hospital (during the school holidays), this seemed to us remarkable. We suggest that it might be due in part at least to the effects of training in sound categorization.

Toby

We turn to the similar but contrasting case of Toby. Toby was as large as Ben, and the same age (five years, eleven months) when first seen. He was not quite as ebullient but had a similar reputation at school in that he was never where he was supposed to be. At initial testing his sound categorization scores were low and almost identical to Ben's: 4, 4, and 5 in the First, Middle, and End Sound conditions respectively. He also seemed distractible when we tested him.

The two boys had identical scores on the memory check,

and on the draw-a-man test. The only major difference between the two was that Toby scored seventeen points less on the E.P.V.T. test (85), which put him at the sixteenth percentile for his age. He also was selected for the training study, but was allocated to Group IV (no training).

Toby changed schools because his mother remarried. The staff at his new school were concerned in a positive way; they carefully monitored his progress, offered secure and supportive teaching with carefully structured programs and specialist remedial help and advice. They sought a cooperative relationship with Toby's mother and tried to ensure that the school offered a secure continuing routine while his home circumstances changed. He settled down very well and integrated in a much more normal way. He appeared to follow a similar drug routine to Ben, and was taken off drugs at the same time.

He was eight years, eight months old at the final testing. He had barely begun to read or spell, and his scores on the standardized reading tests were Neale six years, five months (accuracy), no score (comprehension), and Schonell six years, two months; his Schonell spelling level was five years, seven months.

He was not as bright as Ben, his W.I.S.C./R. scores being 84 (Verbal), 82 (Performance), 81 (Full-Scale). But even when we take his lower intelligence into account and adjust his standardized scores accordingly he is still nineteen months behind on the Schonell reading tests, and of course even further behind on the other tests.

Despite the differences in intelligence, school, and family circumstances there is little doubt that Ben benefited from the training, and that Toby was at a distinct disadvantage; the supportive and remedial teaching that he received did not help improve his ability to categorize words on the basis of sound similarities, and he made virtually no progress using the alphabetic code. Together the two cases suggest quite strongly that a child with a clear organic problem, auditory organization difficulty, and social and behavioral problems can be helped by specific training.

Summary

We have presented four cases as illustrations of the possible influence of skill in sound categorization and of training in sound categorization on learning to read and to spell. These cases show how sound categorization might play a major part in some cases but not in others, and that a child who is trained in sound categorization sometimes fares better in learning to read than a child who is not.

CHAPTER 10

Our Conclusions

It is easy enough to summarize our study. We had a theory about the importance of a skill that children usually acquire before they arrive at school, and that seemed to us very likely to affect the business of learning to read and to write. That skill was the handling of rhyme and alliteration. It is plainly one that involves analyzing phonological segments and thus could affect the child's first experiences with the alphabet, and it is also something we already knew to be particularly difficult for children with learning difficulties.

That was why we arrived at our theory that rhyming and alliteration play an important role in learning to read and to spell. It was the causal theory for which we could find plenty of incidental support but no firm and direct evidence. We thought that there was a definite need for this kind of evidence, positive or negative, for good practical and theoretical reasons. It would tell us more about the difficulties of children with learning difficulties who fail to read and fail to rhyme as well. It would tell us also about normal development, and the links between a child's experiences at home before he goes to school and some very specific skills he must conquer once he gets there. It would tell us a bit more about screening children when they arrive at school in order to alert us to those who might end up in difficulty. And, if intervention were involved, it would also provide some valuable evidence on how children ought to be taught to read.

The project centered around two predictions, but these themselves were shaped by our ideas about how best to test a causal hypothesis about children's development. We had decided that the only satisfactory test of any idea about causes of development would be a combination of the two most commonly used methods—longitudinal prediction and training. Our reasoning was that the two methods have complementary strengths and weaknesses. Longitudinal predictions plot real relationships but ones that are not necessarily causal. Training studies establish causes, but ones that might be artificial and confined to the experiment. So each method gets round the weakness of the other.

Our decision to use them both meant that we had two predictions. One was that a child's ability to detect rhyme and alliteration would be one of the factors that determined how well and how quickly he managed to learn to read and to spell. Thus our longitudinal prediction was that a child's score in our tests of rhyme and alliteration would be closely related to his subsequent progress in reading and spelling, quite independently of his general verbal and intellectual skills. Our second prediction was about the training: we predicted that training children in categorizing sounds should help them to learn to read over and above any other kind of training in categorization.

The main theme of our monograph has been to show how these two predicted results did occur. We think that we have established a causal link between a very specific preschool skill and a particular educational achievement. This specificity is to us one of the most exciting things about our hypothesis and our results. It seems to us that most theories about the effects of preschool experiences and preschool skills on later success or failure in school are of a very general nature. It is, to take a few examples, widely felt that stimulation is important, or that the experiences which a young middle-class child typically has are a particularly suitable preparation for school, or that the experience of a great deal of conversation at home might be a particular help to him when he reaches the classroom. But in all these cases the actual connections between the experiences that are said to be beneficial and what the child must learn at school are left rather vague.

Our hypothesis goes a great deal further than this because it proposes a specific route from a particular type of experience a child typically has before he goes to school and certain skills he must acquire when he gets there. Our proposal is that word games in general and those games that involve rhyme and alliteration in particular give children experience in breaking words up into phonetic segments, and also of grouping together words that are very different from each other but that do have phonetic segments in common. We fasten on this sort of experience because we can make a plausible connection between it and reading. The alphabet involves segmenting words into smaller sounds, and it is easy to see why one kind of segmenting could prepare the child for another.

But this need not be all. Children are taught to group together words that have comon spelling patterns and also share common sounds—groups of words like *fight, might, light,* and *sight.* Rhyming and alliteration games seem to us to be an admirable precursor for that kind of learning too. It is interesting to note that this takes us beyond the task of associating single letters with single phonemes. The relationship between a cluster of letters like *igh* and the sound these letters typically signify is not a simple one of associating single letters with single sounds, for here three letters signify one phoneme. Yet it is easy to see how the categorizing aspect of rhyme and alliteration could prepare a child for the task of spotting how words with common spelling patterns have sounds in common as well.

So much for our central hypothesis and for the support our project produced for it. We can turn now to two implications of our results, both of which are of considerable practical and educational significance. The first concerns the question of learning difficulties in particular, and the second educational and remedial methods in general.

Our starting point was the question of learning difficulties. We had already shown that many backward readers of normal intelligence have great difficulty with the detection of rhyme and alliteration, and we wanted to know more about this difficulty. One thing we wanted to find out was whether the connection between rhyming and reading was a peculiarity of these particular children, or whether, on the contrary, the relationship held true of the normal range of children as well. This is a point we have covered already. But a second and equally important question concerned children with learning difficulties. We wanted to know whether a measure of rhyming and alliteration skills taken *before* children begin to read would make the prediction of reading difficulties more possible.

At the moment it is extremely difficult to take a group of otherwise normal children, children whose intelligence and verbal skills seem quite unimpaired, before they go to school and to work out who among them might eventually experience learning difficulties. We have shown that our measures might make that kind of prediction easier. They are by no means perfect but they do pick out a number of children whose progress in reading and spelling falls well behind the level one would expect from their I.Q. It looks as though failure on our test might be one early indication of learning difficulties. It would of course have to be combined with others. Predicting learning difficulties is bound to be a complicated business.

Predictions are not enough. It does not seem much use to be able to say who will have difficulties at school unless you can at the same time suggest what to do about it. Our view of our measure, sound categorization, is that it carries with it a clear message about how to alleviate any difficulty that it detects. Once we find that something is wrong about sound categorization we are in a good position to put it right. There are really two points to make here. The first concerns preschool experiences. Quite clearly children do usually take to rhyme and alliteration before they go to school, though this is a subject on which we badly need a great deal more research. Quite clearly too the word games and nursery rhymes which involve this auditory organization are part of the normal currency of interactions between parents and their young children, and obviously highly enjoyable interactions at that.

All this suggests very strongly that a child's early experiences with rhymes and alliteration, which we have shown to be so important, may very well be strongly influenced by the parents themselves. They may either encourage or discourage the child's enjoyment and interests in playing with sounds. We cannot from our data say anything about the role of the parents. All we know is that a child's skill in tests of sound categorization at the time that he goes to school plays an important part in his learning to read and to spell. But it seems at least a plausible suggestion, and something that is an obvious candidate for future research, that these skills themselves may be influenced by the parents, and it would surely do no harm to suggest that parents encourage their children's interest in rhymes and word games.

There is little doubt that this would help the normal run of children. Whether it would work with children who otherwise would eventually experience learning difficulties is another matter. As we have shown these children often find rhymes and alliteration extraordinarily opaque. All the signs now are that this block is there from very early on in life. In that case this barrier might be too· high for parents to surmount with the normal sort of encouragement and incentive. For these children we might be forced to turn to particular remedial methods.

We do have a few suggestions to make about such methods. Our project suggests that teaching sound categorization alone to children already at school does have an effect on·progress in reading and spelling. But that effect is vastly amplified if the training is accompanied by experience with alphabetic letters. In other words, children who are already being taught to read are helped even more if the sound categories are encapsulated in alphabetic letters too. We must be cautious about this recommendation, because it comes from training conditions that were rather unusual. Our training always involved one teacher with one child, so we cannot say for certain that it would work or would work as well if groups of children or whole class-rooms were involved. But the success of this method, which involved letters as well as training in sound categories, was so strong that it is difficult to believe that it would not have a marked effect in classrooms as well as in individual sessions.

Thus our project has done three things. It has established a specific causal link between a preschool skill and reading and spelling. It has shown one effective way of predicting success in reading and spelling, independent of intelligence. It has suggested ways not only of predicting how well children might do, but also of helping them over the barriers that our tests seem to identify. Together these three points may help us understand more clearly some of the things that are involved in learning to read and in failing to learn to read. They should also, we trust, help the group of children whose problems originally prompted our project, children with learning difficulties.

References

Alegria, J.; Pignot, E.; and Morais, J. 1982. "Phonetic Analysis of Speech and Memory Codes in Beginning Readers." *Memory and Cognition* 10:451–56.

Audley, R. J. 1976. "Reading Difficulties: The Importance of Basic Research in Solving Practical Problems." Presidential Address: Section J, British Association for the Advancement of Science. Lancaster.

Bradley, L. 1980. *Assessing Reading Difficulties: A Diagnostic and Remedial Approach.* London and Basingstoke: Macmillan Education.

———. 1982. "Alliteration, Rhyming, Reading and Spelling in Young Children and Backward Readers." Abstracts B.P.S. London Conference. *Bulletin of the British Psychological Society* 35:18.

Bradley, L., and Bryant, P. E. 1978. "Difficulties in Auditory Organisation as a Possible Cause of Reading Backwardness." *Nature* 271:746–47.

———. 1979. "The Independence of Reading and Spelling in Backward and Normal Readers." *Developmental Medicine and Child Neurology* 21:504–14.

———. 1983. "Categorising Sounds and Learning to Read: A Causal Connexion." *Nature* 301:419–21.

Bruce, D. J. 1964. "The Analysis of Word Sounds." *British Journal of Educational Psychology* 34:158–70.

Bryant, P. E. 1981. "Training and Logic." In *Intelligence and Learning,* ed. M. P. Friedman, J. P. Das, and N. O'Connor. N.A.T.O. Conference Series. Series III Human Factors. New York: Plenum Press.

Bryant, P. E., and Bradley, L. 1980. "Why Children Sometimes Write Words Which They Cannot Read." In *Cognitive Processes in Spelling,* ed. U. Frith. London: Academic Press.

Bullock, A. 1975. *A Language for Life.* The Report of Inquiry Appointed by the Secretary of State for Education and Science. London: H.M.S.O.

Calfee, R.; Chapman, R.; and Venezky, R. 1972. "How a Child

Needs to Think to Learn to Read." In *Cognition in Learning and Memory*, ed. L. W. Gregg. New York: Wiley.

Chukovsky, K. 1963. *From Two to Five*. Berkeley and Los Angeles: University of California Press.

Chukovsky, K. I. 1956. "Ot dvukh do pyati." In *The Psychology of Preschool Children*, ed. A. V. Zaporozhets and D. B. Elkonin. 1971. Cambridge, Mass.: MIT Press.

Clarke, A. M., and Clarke, A. D. B. 1976. *Early Experience: Myth and Evidence*. London: Open Books.

Coltheart, M. 1983. "Phonological Awareness: A Preschool Precursor of Success in Reading." *Nature* 301:370.

Doctor, E. A., and Coltheart, M. 1980. "Children's Use of Phonological Encoding when Reading for Meaning." *Memory and Cognition* 8:195–209.

Douglas, J. W. B.; Ross, J. M.; and Simpson, H. R. 1968. *All Our Future*. London: Peter Davies.

Fox, B., and Routh, D. K. 1975. "Analysing Spoken Language into Words, Syllables and Phonemes: A Developmental Study." *Journal of Psycholinguistic Research* 4:331–42.

Frith, U. 1970. "Studies in Pattern Detection in Normal and Autistic Children: Reproduction and Production of Colour Sequences." *Journal of Experimental Child Psychology* 10:120–35.

Frith, U., and Snowling, M. 1983. "Reading for Meaning and Reading for Sound in Autistic and Dyslexic Children." *British Journal of Developmental Psychology* 1:329–42.

Gleitman, L. R., and Rozin, P. 1977. "The Structure and Acquisition of Reading. Relations between Orthographies and the Structure of Language." In *Toward a Psychology of Reading*, ed. A. S. Reber and D. L. Scarborough. New York: Lawrence Erlbaum Associates.

Goldstein, D. M. 1976. "Cognitive-linguistic Functioning and Learning to Read in Preschoolers." *Journal of Educational Psychology* 68:680–88.

Golinkoff, R. M. 1978. "Phonemic Awareness Skills and Reading Achievement." In *The Acquisition of Reading*, ed. F. B. Murray and J. J. Pikulski. Baltimore: University Park Press.

Grieve, R.; Tunmer, W. E.; and Pratt, C. 1980. "An Introduction to the Study of Language Awareness in Children." In *Language Awareness in Chidren*, ed. C. Pratt and R. Grieve. Vol. 7 of *Education Research and Perspectives*. Nedlands: University of Western Australia.

Hakes, D. T.; Evans, J.; and Tunmer, W. 1980. *The Development of Metalinguistic Abilities in Children*. Berlin: Springer Verlag.

Hermelin, B., and O'Connor, N. 1970. *Psychological Experiments with Autistic Children.* Oxford: Pergamon.

Hirsch-Pasek, K.; Gleitman, R.; and Gleitman, H. 1978. "What Did the Brain Say to the Mind? A Study of the Detection and Report of Ambiguity." In *The Child's Conception of Language,* ed. A. Sinclair, R. J. Jarvella, and W. J. M. Levelt. Berlin: Springer Verlag.

Horgan, D. 1981. "Learning to Tell Jokes: A Case Study of Metalinguistic Abilities." *Journal of Child Language* 8:217–24.

Lenel, J. C., and Cantor, J. H. 1981. "Rhyme Recognition and Phonemic Perception in Young Children." *Journal of Psycholinguistic Research* 10:57–68.

Liberman, I. Y., and Shankweiler, D. 1976. "Speech, the Alphabet and Teaching to Read." In *Theory and Practice of Early Reading,* ed. L. Resnick and P. Weaver. Hillsdale, N.J.: Lawrence Erlbaum Associates.

Liberman, I. Y.; Shankweiler, D.; Liberman, A. M.; Fowler, C.; and Fischer, F. W. 1978. "Phonetic Segmentation and Recoding in the Beginning Reader. In *Toward a Psychology of Reading,* ed. A. S. Reber and D. L. Scarborough. New York: Lawrence Erlbaum Associates.

Lundberg, I. 1978. "Aspects of Linguistic Awareness Related to Reading." In *The Child's Conception of Language,* ed. A. Sinclair, R. J. Jarvella, and W. J. M. Levelt. Berlin: Springer Verlag.

Lundberg, I.; Olofsson, A.; and Wall, S. 1981. "Reading and Spelling Skills in the First School Years Predicted from Phonemic Awareness Skills in Kindergarten." *Scandinavian Journal of Psychology* 21:159–73.

Maxwell, A. E. 1959. "A Factor Analysis of the Wechsler Intelligence Scale for Children." *British Journal of Educational Psychology* 29:237–41.

Morais, J.; Cary, L.; Alegria, J.; and Bertelson, P. 1979. "Does Awareness of Speech as a Sequence of Phones Arise Spontaneously?" *Cognition* 7:323–31.

Naidoo, S. 1972. *Specific Dyslexia.* London: Pitman.

National Foundation for Educational Research in England and Wales. 1970. *Mathematics Attainment Test B.* Windsor: National Foundation for Educational Research.

Nesdale, A. R.; Herriman, M.; and Tunmer, W. 1980. "The Development of Phonological Awareness." In *Language Awareness in Children,* ed. C. Pratt and R. Grieve. Vol. 7 of *Education Research and Perspectives.* Nedlands: University of Western Australia.

O'Connor, N., and Hermelin, B. 1963. *Speech and Thought in Severe Subnormality*. Oxford: Pergamon.

Olofsson, A., and Lundberg, I. 1983. "Can Phonemic Awareness be Trained in Kindergarten?" *Scandinavian Journal of Psychology* 24:35–44.

Perin, D. 1983. "Phonemic Segmentation and Spelling." *British Journal of Psychology* 74:129–44.

Read, C. 1978. "Children's Awareness of Language, with Emphasis on Sound Systems." In *The Child's Conception of Language,* ed. A. Sinclair, R. J. Jarvella, and W. J. M. Levelt. Berlin: Springer Verlag.

Rozin, P., and Gleitman, L. R. 1978. "The Structure and Acquisition of Reading II: The Reading Process and the Acquisition of the Alphabetic Principle." In *Toward a Psychology of Reading,* ed. A. S. Reber and D. L. Scarborough. New York: Lawrence Erlbaum Associates.

Savin, H. B. 1972. "What the Child Knows about Speech When He Starts to Learn to Read." In *Language by Ear and by Eye,* ed. J. F. Kavanagh and I. G. Mattingly. Cambridge, Mass.: MIT Press.

Schonell, F. 1950. *Diagnostic and Attainment Testing in Teaching.* London and Edinburgh: Oliver and Boyd.

Schonell, F., and Goodacre, E. 1971. *The Psychology and Teaching of Reading.* 5th ed. London and Edinburgh: Oliver and Boyd.

Sinclair, A.; Jarvella, R. J.; and Levelt, W. J. M. 1978. *The Child's Conception of Language.* Berlin: Springer Verlag.

Slobin, D. I. 1978. *Studies of Child Language Development.* New York: Holt, Rinehart, and Winston.

Snowling, M. J. 1980. "The Development of Grapheme-Phoneme Correspondence in Normal and Dyslexic Readers." *Journal of Experimental Child Psychology* 29:294–305.

Snowling, M., and Frith, U. 1981. "The Use of Sound, Shape and Orthographic Cues in Early Reading." *British Journal of Psychology* 72:83–88.

Snowling, M., and Perin, D. 1982. "The Development of Phoneme Segmentation Skills in Young Children." In *The Acquisition of Symbolic Skills,* ed. J. Sloboda and D. A. Rogers. New York: Plenum Press.

Stevenson, H. W.; Stigler, J. W.; Lucker, G. W.; Lee, S.Y.; Hsu, C. C.; and Kitamura, S. "Reading Disabilities: The Case of Chinese, Japanese and English." *Child Development* 53:1164–81.

Vellutino, F. R. 1979. *Dyslexia: Theory and Research.* Cambridge Mass.: MIT Press.

Vihman, M. M. 1981. "Phonology and the Development of the Lexicon: Evidence from Children's Errors." *Journal of Child Language* 8:239–64.

Walk, R. 1981. *Perceptual Development.* Monterey, Calif.: Brooks/Cole Publishing Co.

Zhurova, L. Y. 1973. "The Development of Analysis of Words into Their Sounds by Preschool Children." In *Studies of Child Language Development,* ed. C. A. Ferguson and D. I. Slobin. New York: Holt, Rinehart, and Winston.

www.ingramcontent.com/pod-product-compliance
Lightning Source LLC
Chambersburg PA
CBHW020707270326
41928CB00005B/306